Design:Japan

Design:Japan

PHOTOGRAPHY BY MICHAEL FREEMAN
TEXT BY MICHIKO RICO NOSÉ

MITCHELL BEAZLEY

Design : Japan
Photography by **Michael Freeman**
Text by **Michiko Rico Nosé**

First published in 2004 by Mitchell Beazley,
an imprint of Octopus Publishing Group Ltd,
2–4 Heron Quays, London E14 4JP

© Octopus Publishing Group Ltd 2004
Photographs © Michael Freeman 2003

ISBN 1 84000 779 6

A CIP record of this book is available
from the British Library

Commissioning Editor: **Mark Fletcher**
Managing Editor: **Hannah Barnes-Murphy**
Executive Art Editor: **Auberon Hedgecoe**
Project Editor: **Peter Taylor**
Translation: **Rina Takayama/Chris Toker**
Design: **Pocknell**
Production: **Gary Hayes**

Set in Bliss
Printed and bound in China by
Toppan Printing Company Limited

To order this book as a gift or an incentive contact
Mitchell Beazley on 020 7531 8481

CONTENTS

There are three terms in modern Japanese design that go a long way towards explaining the current scene: "Japanese style", "non-concept", and "freedom". These terms, which may be slightly surprising to Westerners, share a common influence, namely the changed circumstances wrought by the collapse of the bubble economy of the 1980s.

True Japanese style means to us, as in the West, the traditional components. These were largely abandoned during the period of Japanese high-speed economic development in 1955–73. In its place, Western design became mainstream, and housing styles followed suit. But then, during the bubble era, "Japanese style" started to appear in restaurants and commercial contexts as a design motif.

Most of today's new designers have little experience of real Japanese style. The *tatami* mat room, for example, which was traditionally a part of individual homes, can now hardly be found in this context. Instead, it has survived more successfully in restaurants, many of which have become, in a sense, cultural repositories.

Modern Japanese grow up with commercialized national traditions that form no part of their home life, so it is hardly surprising that instead they digest their childhood memories and reconstruct them in design. This Westernized "Japanese style" is now apparently Japanese culture, and it gives us a kind of nostalgic feeling – a nostalgia for a short, basically colonial, period.

Japan used to copy the West, and now those parts of traditional lifestyle which have not been washed away have returned to take their place in a modern vocabulary of design, albeit one laced with irony. Even young Japanese who have no experience of *tatami* mat rooms and the like in everyday life can distinguish fake from real. Dharma, a restaurant designed by BBA International (page 126), actually looks as if it had been designed by a foreigner, as it is in a deliberately incorrect "Japanese style". Indeed, misunderstanding is an intentional and important factor in the designer's concept, a new twist on the ambiguity that has always played a part in our culture and design.

Opposite page: Making cakes at Moph, a café created by Claudio Colucci, an Italian designer who came to Japan in 1998.
Right: A word is transformed into sculpture in The Terrace, the office building of architect Ken Yokogawa.

We have always utilized our folk art, redesigning its artefacts according to the dynamics of contemporary living spaces. This approach has, we Japanese believe, set it apart from the traditional crafts of other Asian countries. The Japanese have a talent for interpreting from reimportation, yet at the same time are good at keeping their distance from the rest of the world.

Another Western influence during the bubble period was the "concept", which quickly became the buzzword of high design. The consumer accepted it as an underlying quality of an enormous range of goods, and was happy to embrace the creator's intention, impressed by the usually spurious depth that it offered. All that was fine while the economy was in good form. But now it has clearly changed.

I have tried in this book to analyse a Japan which is developing design skills during an economic recession. It is a fascinating time. With less money to spend, consumers focus more seriously on what they really want. They are less prepared to spend income on often vague, even meaningless ideas, and for the new generation of designers, the concept has to follow the product, not pull it.

A good example of a "non-concept" brand is Muji. At present, the fashion designer Yoji Yamamoto and one of the designers introduced in this book, Toshihiko Suzuki, are contributing their work, yet Muji is not pushing their identities, maintaining its policy of anonymity. This is the era of *not* relying on the designer's name. The driving force that propels Japanese design is its economic status, not celebrity.

"Japanese style" is now revived by a generation that has not actually experienced it in everyday life, creating a link between past and present. The present Japanese idea of "freedom" exists in its traditional sense and also in the sense of consumers' freedom to follow their individual tastes and needs, rather than an invented concept. This is helped by the timespan inherent in the reworking of Japanese style, the bridging of fundamental tradition and temporary fashion. With "concept" removed from the equation, designers are now more than ever addressing real and specific consumer needs. In the leaner times of these post-boom years, design in Japan is informed by a new realism.

Makoto Shin Watanabe

Architect (ADH Architects)

25/11/1950,

Gunma Prefecture, Japan

Yoko Kinoshita

Architect (ADH Architects)

7/2/1956

Tokyo, Japan

Watanabe After studying in Venice and completing a Masters programme at both Kyoto University and Harvard University, Watanabe worked with Cambridge Seven Associates and Arata Isozaki & Associates before establishing ADH Architects with Yoko Kinoshita. He is presently a professor at Hosei University and has acted as a visiting critic at the University of Texas.

Guen Bertheau-Suzuki

Architect/Designer

17/8/1956

Paris, France

After studying in Belgium and Tokyo, Bertheau-Suzuki worked with architects Biro & Fernier (Paris) and later Arata Isozaki & Associates. He is currently a visiting professor at Nihon University. Recent architectural projects include the GEN distillery and leisure facilities and the Toshin building. He has undertaken interior design for the Krediet Bank in Tokyo and Cartier's Japan Service Centre and has decorated for Issey Miyake fashion exhibitions.

Claudio Colucci

Designer

5/7/1965

Locarno, Switzerland

After studying in Geneva, Paris, and the USA, Colucci worked with Ron Arad and Nigel Coates in London, and Pascal Mourgue and Thompson Multimedia (under Philippe Starck) in Paris, forming Radi Designers in 1994. He began work in Japan with IDÉE in 1996 and opened the Radi Designers Tokyo office in 1998, collaborating with Philippe Starck for 7/Eleven. CCDESIGN was established in 2002, with offices in Tokyo and Paris.

Akihito Fumita

Interior Designer

13/7/1962

Osaka Prefecture, Japan

After graduating from the Osaka University of Arts, Fumita joined RIC DESIGN. He established FUMITA DESIGN OFFICE in Osaka in 1995 and moved to Tokyo in 1999. Major projects include Natural Body, the Nissan Ginza Gallery, the Nissan booth at the Tokyo Motor Show (2001, 2002), and the Room in Bloom at Osaka Takashimaya.

Yasuhiro Hamano

Lifestyle Producer

22/7/1941

Kyoto, Japan

After studying film production and direction, Hamano established Hamano Institute Co., Ltd (now Hamano Institute Inc.) and in 1992 formed Team Hamano. Recent projects include the construction of OmniQuarter, production of hhstyle.com and Arita Pottery Club, and establishment of the mini theatre complex planning company Q. He has created a number of publications, such as *Digital City* and *TEAM HAMANO & PROJECTS*.

Yasuhiro Harada

Producer

15/5/1963

Osaka Prefecture, Japan

Producer for Cube. Major projects include Club Zen, Cube Hatago, Azool, and the dining lounge Souen (Aoyama).

Kinoshita Having completed a Masters at Harvard University, Kinoshita worked for Shozo Uchii Architect and Associates before co-founding ADH Architects. She is a lecturer at the Shibaura Institute of Technology and Nihon University and has acted as a visiting critic at the University of Texas.

Designing for the non-nuclear family is our challenge.

Peace.

What you see is not necessarily what you get.

It should be possible to discover Japanese DNA within contemporary expression. Shouldn't it?

Natural restoration. The resurrection of vernacular design. Human scale.

As the company name "Cube" indicates, our goal is not only to create spaces, but to realize a wide variety of things in the third dimension. We hope that through our planning and production we can present one form of "Japanese style" to the world.

Yukio Hashimoto

Interior Designer

13/3/1962

Aichi Prefecture, Japan

After graduating from the Aichi Prefectural University of Arts, Hashimoto joined Super Potato Co., Ltd. Head of Hashimoto Yukio Design Studio, his recent projects have included the restaurants Otooto, Shu-an, Azumiya (Ginza and Aoyama), and Kamonka Tameike Sanno, as well as the boutique BEAMS HOUSE. He is presently a lecturer at the Joshibi University of Art and Design and Aichi Prefectural University of Arts.

Masaaki Hiromura

Designer

19/8/1954

Aichi Prefecture, Japan

Hiromura joined the Ikko Tanaka Design Studio in 1977 and received the Japan Sign Design Association Award in 1983. In 1988, he established the Hiromura Design Office Inc., Tokyo. Recent honours include the 2001 Good Design Award, and the CS Design Gold Award (2002).

Hisae Igarashi

Designer

Tokyo, Japan

Igarashi joined the Kuramata Design Office after graduating from the Kuwasawa Institute of Design and in 1993 opened Igarashi Design Studio. Representative works include the café Royal (2001), a boutique for TSUMORI CHISATO (1995) and the collective housing project RYU.GAN.SOU (Tokyo Collaboration, 1994).

Richard Scott Isaac

Artist

30/10/1963

Wakefield, England

A self-taught and trained artist, Isaac's work is permanently displayed throughout Japan in numerous private collections.

Michimasa Kawaguchi

Architect

23/9/1952

Hyogo Prefecture, Japan

A self-taught architect, Kawaguchi's projects such as Metrogate, Black Housing, and the Atami Tantei villa often incorporate a traditional Japanese sensibility. He was awarded the third UD Prize for urban architecture in 1992 and the Kawaguchi City Machikado Spot Prize for design in 1999.

Koh Kitayama

Architect

14/7/1950

Kagawa Prefecture, Japan

While studying within the Yokohama National University architectural program, Kitayama established the group studio WORKSHOP. He is currently a professor at Yokohama National University and runs Koh Kitayama + architecture WORKSHOP. Major works include the Katta Public General Hospital, the Shimouma Townhouse, and OmniQuarter.

My goal is not to design material, but to design an ambience.

Design begins with organizing.

Design is love.

Nothing is old in Tokyo, except the old people.

Beautiful light creates beautiful space; beautiful space creates beautiful people. The discovery of beauty gives birth to everything.

The act of creating requires believing in yourself despite your doubts.

Yosei Kiyono

Restaurant Producer

1963

Tokyo, Japan

Kiyono has designed over 200 different restaurants, including Hinode Shokudo (Aoyama, 2000). He has also worked with Japan Railways in designing lunchboxes.

Mark Dytham

Architect (Klein Dytham Architecture)

4/9/1964

Northamptonshire, England

Astrid Klein

Architect (Klein Dytham Architecture)

22/3/1962

Varese, Italy

Dytham After gaining a BA in Architecture at Newcastle University and an MA at London's Royal College of Art, Dytham worked for Skidmore Owings & Merrill in Chicago and London. In 1988, he won a travel scholarship to Tokyo, where he worked with Toyo Ito Architects & Associates. In 1991, he co-founded Klein Dytham Architecture. He is an assistant professor at Tokyo Science University and a lecturer at Hosei and Tsukuba universities.

Kengo Kuma

Architect

8/8/1954, Kanagawa Prefecture, Japan

In 1979, Kuma was awarded an MA by the University of Tokyo. He was a visiting scholar at Columbia in 1985–6. In 1987, he established the Spatial Design Studio, followed by Kengo Kuma & Associates in 1990. He is currently a professor in the Faculty of Environmental Information at Keio University. Recent projects include the Baiso Temple (Tokyo), the Tsukiji Fishmarket urban project (Tokyo), and Bamboo House III (Beijing, China).

Masayuki Kurokawa

Architect

4/4/1937, Aichi Prefecture, Japan

After graduating from a doctoral course in architecture at Waseda University, Kurokawa established the Kurokawa Masayuki Architect Studio in 1967. His works are exhibited in the permanent design collection of the Museum of Modern Art in New York and the Denver Art Museum. In 2001, he established Designtope Co., Ltd, with the aim of supporting innovative design. He is presently a professor at the Kanazawa College of Art.

Tsutomu Kurokawa

Interior Designer

25/5/1962, Aichi Prefecture, Japan

Kurokawa began designing in 1987 with the company Super Potato, and in 1992 established H. Design Associates, followed by OUT.Design in 2000. His work focuses on space design, furnishing, and lighting. Recent projects include space design for Sage de Cret (Aoyama, 2002) and UNDER COVER MEN'S (Aoyama, 1999) and furniture such as Lenorat (LED lamp, 2002) and Papima (chair, 2001).

Keiko Matsumoto

Accessory Designer

23/7/1967, Tokyo, Japan

After completing studies in painting at the Tama University of Art, Matsumoto travelled to Europe. While working in art restoration, she also creates fabric collages that are exhibited annually at Gallery K in Ginza. In 1992 her cloth, wire, and paper installations were exhibited in Zurich, Milan, Paris, and Düsseldorf. A self-taught accessory designer, Matsumoto began sale of her works in 1993.

"Past/future", "Imaginary/real", "modern/classic"... I would like to be someone who instills value from a neutral viewpoint by finding new possibilities in the interstices between opposites.

Klein After undergraduate studies in Strasbourg and an MA at London's Royal College of Art, Klein won a travel scholarship to Tokyo, where she worked for Toyo Ito Architects & Associates. In 1991, she co-founded Klein Dytham Architecture. She is a lecturer at Keio and Tsukuba universities.

Installation? Branding? Architecture? Furniture? Advertising? Landscape? Product design? How do we define what we do? Should we? Why worry – it's the smile that counts!

Material is the essence of architecture. It is the material itself that forms the exterior instead of a thinly applied finish.

Design is poetry of form and materials and light. If design impresses us, then this trumps all logic and utility.

To me, design is creating something normal that has never been seen before.

Applying the concept of simplicity allows us to show how much we can subtract.

Yoshihisa Matsuzawa

photographed with Masatomi Fujimaki
and Hana Nagamoto

Restaurant Development Producer

12/9/1968, Niigata, Japan

Matsuzawa began working at BBA International through Nittaku Enterprises. Major projects include Dharma and café NOLITA. After completion of the J-pop Café Odaiba, he is now working on the discotheque/salon J-pop Café Tapei.

Takeshi Nagasaki

Artist/Gardener

15/7/1970, Nara Prefecture,

Japan

After studying at the Tokyo National University of Fine Arts, Nagasaki began working with woodcut printing and sculpture, and later became a self-taught gardener. In 1997 he started N-tree, and in 2000 won third prize in the Kawagoe Tea Ceremony Room Design Competition. He produced the small garden GARDENS NOW in 2002 and exhibits woodcut prints and wood sculpture annually at Tenshin-an.

Ichiro Shiomi

Interior Designer **(spinoff ltd)**

1962

Hyogo Prefecture, Japan

Etsuko Yamamoto

Interior Designer **(spinoff ltd)**

1969

Aichi Prefecture, Japan

Shimi After graduating from the Osaka University of Arts Department of Design, Shiomi joined the Nobu Interior Design Office. In 1992 he established spinoff ltd. Major projects include XEX Daikanyama, and Soup Stock Tokyo (Akasaka, etc.).

Toshihiko Suzuki

Architect

23/7/1958, Tokyo, Japan

After studying architecture at Kogakuin University, Suzuki was awarded a scholarship by the French government to train with public urban developers EPA Marne. After returning to Japan, Suzuki worked on the company's French, Dutch, Belgian, and Bulgarian projects. He continued his studies in Kyoto and Tokyo, researching lightweight materials and structures. He is presently a professor at the Tohoko University of Art and Design.

Katsu Umebayashi

Architect

26/10/1963, Kyoto, Japan

After graduating from the Osaka University of Arts, Umebayashi joined Shin Takamatsu & Associates. In 1994, he established FOB Association, followed by FOB HOMES in 1999, with Mitsue Matsunaga and Shingo Fujiwaki. He has served as a lecturer at the Kyoto University of Art and Design, Ritsumeikan University and Seika University, and is presently a lecturer at the Tokyo Metropolitan University.

Ken Yokogawa

Architect

9/7/1948, Tokyo, Japan

After graduating from Nihon University and working with Masayuki Kurokawa Architect & Associates, Yokogawa established Ken Yokogawa Architect & Associates, Inc. Representative works include Glass House, The Center of Environmental Science in Saitama (CESS) and Tunnel house. He is presently a professor at the Nihon University College of Science and Technology.

Originality is born from the clues laid by our predecessors. Viewing a variety of things is key to creating.

I work in the conflict zone between obstinate white and innocent black.

Yamamoto Yamamoto has worked with is architects & associates and spinoff ltd.

Producing, yet not overproducing, things for a comfortable ambience.

Spatial furniture, product-like space.

Creating something in proximity with the body, an ecological environment.

I wish to project the traditional Japanese concept of "delicacy" into the culture of today.

WORK

Previous page, opposite page, and right: Images from Q Front, a giant digital screen that forms the facade of a building in Tokyo.

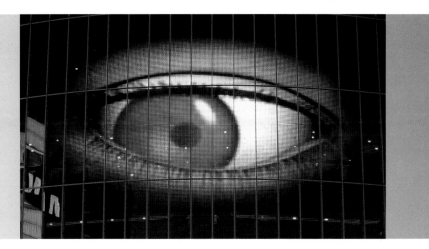

These days, Japanese designers and architects are well aware of the need for innovation and style in the workplace. During the bubble economy of the 1980s, however, they focused their attentions elsewhere. Offices, with their fluorescent lights and plain grey metal desks, were doing just fine. Everyone was working hard and enjoying their work, so they left well enough alone and concentrated on creating things and places for entertainment. Aesthetics were associated with leisure time; art and style were the rewards for hard work and financial gain.

But the current economic climate has led to a re-evaluation of priorities. Employers need to encourage creativity and comfort at work, and designers are being enlisted in this enterprise. And it's not just the offices and office buildings that are being rethought: train stations and even financial data screens are also being redesigned to be more attractive and interesting.

A booming economy encourages innovation, but a difficult economy requires it. Japanese designers and architects are playing their part in creating comfortable environments that can be enjoyed by people in difficult circumstances. And the hope is that the infusion of aesthetics and creativity into the workplace will, in turn, help the economy.

Q Front IT (information technology) is changing the way we see the world. Not only is the workplace inundated with new technology, Japanese designers are using it to help redesign the workplace itself.

Q Front is a vast, 450-square-metre digital screen built into the façade of a building in Shibuya, Tokyo. An enormous media installation, Q Front serves as a window for those inside and a constantly changing display for those outside. Yasuhiro Hamano, the planner of this screen development, describes Q Front as urban media's new billboard.

Trends emanate from the Shibuya section of Tokyo, it is both the centre of youth culture and fashion and of IT business, which is growing with the development of broadband and information technology. It is an intensely urban area – it only has 1.9 million inhabitants, but the JR railway line brings in more than 420,000 people a day on average.

Q Front is located just in front of Hachi-koh, a famous landmark statue in Tokyo – a visible and busy spot. The screen also benefits from being sited near a pedestrian crossing. While people wait to cross the road, they look up. Architect Koh Kitayama was part of the project from its inception; at an initial brainstorming session in Hamano's office, Kitayama first proposed his idea to make the curtain wall of the building's facade a huge screen.

It was constructed in December 1999 at a cost of 5.7 billion yen. In keeping with the spirit and look of Shibuya, the planners created a building that embodies media – both inside and out. Behind the digital facade, the building teems with magazines, game software, DVDs, videos, CDs, and young people. Starbucks is on the first and second floor and stays open until 2 am for the late-night crowd. Other tenants include Tsutaya, Japan's biggest CD-rental company, a school for multimedia design, and a highly original modern cuisine restaurant. Taken as a whole, the entire structure is a media lighthouse sending out information to the world via a giant digital screen.

Above and overleaf: The interactive screen of Bloomberg ICE, a financial news and data screen with a twist.

Bloomberg ICE Another new Japanese landmark, the Marunouchi Building (see also pages 145 and 156), features a digital billboard designed by Klein Dytham Architecture (Mark Dytham and Astrid Klein) that proclaims the marriage of digital technology and design. The building is located in the central Marunouchi business district in Tokyo, near to the train station. Mitsubishi-jisho sekkei inc., the company that is developing a number of blocks in this area including the Marunouchi building, is hoping to turn the broad boulevard that leads from the railway station to the Outer Palace Garden into a Japanese version of the Champs-Elysées.

For most people, financial news and data is a dry affair. But Dytham has turned numbers into design for his client, the global news and information provider Bloomberg. His collaborator was Toshio Iwai, an artist who is one of the world's leading digital interface designers. Dytham says that Iwai helped him with the "demystification" of computers and data.

This is no ordinary billboard. As the name "ICE" (Interactive Communication Experience) expresses, the design is pure and very cool. The architects describe the screen as like an icicle hanging from the ceiling – "a pure white element that allows clouds of information to condense". The ICE is linked to three computers, and when there is no one near, its 5.0m x 3.5m (16ft x 11ft) glass wall shows real-time financial data – but in a dramatic new way: if the stock figures are up, they appear to swell and rise; if they are down, they plunge down the screen.

Once you approach the screen, there are infrared sensors that are hidden behind the wall that detect your presence and you can begin to interact with the data. Ambiguous menus scroll down the three-colour, 80,000-pixel screen, giving you options to play games including, among others, digital wave (an interactive drawing game), digital volleyball (an interactive ball game), or a digital harp (a virtual musical instrument). According to a staff member of Klein Dytham, "At this moment, I can safely say that there is no space more interactive than this on this planet."

The tiles you see on the ICE display are made from a "memory gel" called Technogel. They are the result of a partnership between Klein Dytham and the Italian manufacturer that produces the material. This gel is conventionally used in wheelchair seats and surgical pillows to provide shock absorption and insulation. Klein Dytham decided to use the material here because of its tactile softness. The designers first used Technogel in a collaboration with the Italian material sponsor for the "Interni in Piazza" exhibition in Milan, a two-week design convention and exhibition, with different "rooms" installed in the main piazzas of Milan. For the exhibition, Klein Dytham created "Gumi Bath", an enormous duck shaped from the gelatinous but sturdy material. The title of the piece is a play on the candy it resembles, used

to make "Gumi Bears", "Gumi Worms", and other chewy creatures. "We always try to use new and different materials," say the Klein Dytham partners. "If we use the same material repeatedly, it becomes just a recipe, and the design suffers."

For a century, the original Marunouchi office building had occupied this site, becoming in recent years an expensive irrelevance. The land it occupied soared in value during the eighties, yet it no longer fulfilled modern office requirements. Finally, at a cost of 6.2 billion yen, this famous site was completely gutted and refurbished, opening in September 2002, and attracting corporate tenants like Bloomberg.

Although Marunouchi has traditionally been a business district, the city was keen to attract retail customers to the area for shopping and entertainment, and encouraged a dual-use design. In addition to offices, the new building now houses restaurants, fashion and lifestyle shops, as well as display space for new product launches. The location is sufficiently close to Ginza to stimulate, the city hopes, a new shopping corridor.

Nissan Ginza Gallery Here at Nissan Ginza Gallery, information technology, advertising, and gallery exhibitions merge in a sly, new way. While Nissan values the internet as a tool that can transmit information about its product all over the world, regardless of place, time, and nationality, they also need a place to display their goods – a car is tangible, after all.

Akihito Fumita, the designer of this showroom, wanted to display cars like jewellery in a showcase. Ginza, the luxurious commercial heart of Tokyo, is the perfect home for such a project. With space at a premium, Fumita had to use his ingenuity to design a showroom that created the illusion of a larger space. By using the same material to line both the wall and the floor (with curves hiding the borderlines), Fumita has created a space in which the visitor's sense of distance is clouded. A horizontal "flow" of aluminium spandrel graces the entranceway. Embossed stainless steel panels absorb the noise. This is an imaginative, thoughtful space.

Nissan Ginza Gallery has become an extremely popular destination, attracting over 600,000 people a year – some 1,700 a day, on average – not a minor accomplishment considering its competitive location. One reason for the showroom's success is that, together

Above: The reception area of Nissan Ginza Gallery. *Opposite page:* The gallery-like showroom. *Overleaf:* The futuristic product information centre.

with Q Front and Bloomberg ICE, it has become one of Tokyo's design landmarks and consequently it is now one of the most popular places to arrange to meet people.

In 1999 Nissan launched a "Revival Plan" to combat falling profits and secure the company's future. As part of the plan, one of the biggest corporate restructurings ever seen in Japan, Nissan's design department sponsored a competition to improve their brand identity. Six young architects and interior designers submitted designs to build a gallery, and Fumita's design was the winner. The requirement from the Nissan design department was that the space had to have a kind of "Japanese DNA" and be conducive to selling their cars.

Carlos Ghosn, Nissan's chief executive officer, wanted to make sure that visitors to the gallery would also be able to get specific information about Nissan's cars. In a space-age room on the mezzanine level of the gallery (illustrated overleaf) a visitor can absorb such information. So far, Nissan's plan has been a conspicuous success. In the first year after it was announced, the company's after-tax profits were 331.1 billion yen.

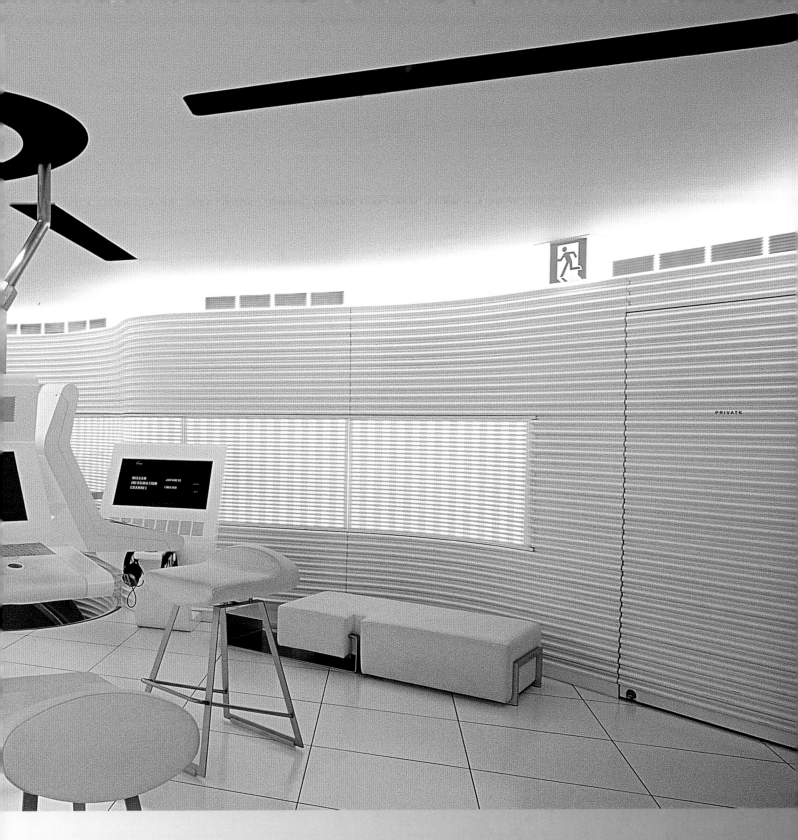

Fumita's design embraces deception. What looks hard may, in fact, be soft; what looks cold may be warm. In the entranceway of the gallery, for example, a material with a subtle relief pattern looks like it is made from cold metal, but when you touch it, you realize that it is made from a soft material. It is, in fact, moulded PVC, an organic resin. (Polyvinyl chloride is often used as building material, but it is rarely used for a wall.) Innovative, ingenious, and deceptive – Fumita's gallery is a sly achievement.

Beacon Communications The offices of the advertising agency Beacon Communications were also designed by Klein Dytham Architecture. A new company, Beacon Communications was formed by the merger of three major agencies. Its offices occupy four floors in a building located in front of Meguro station in Tokyo. No pillars obstruct the 60m x 15m (197ft x 49ft) floors, and to encourage interaction between the 320 employees, the designers were asked to create an open-plan office, rather than following the current trend toward cubicles. There are no enclosed private offices here – even for the directors.

A clever freestanding partition resembling a long ribbon is used to define and redefine spaces within the larger structure – joining or separating the conference rooms, for example. Beacon decided upon assigning a "theme" to each floor. The themes are Woman, Man, Family, and Community. On the Family floor, the ribbon-like partition is made of wood, and the conference room is designed like a kitchen. On the Man floor, the partition is made of stainless steel. On the Woman floor, the partition circumscribes a conference room positioned next to a beauty parlour. The styles of the meeting are of course affected by the design of the space.

Above: The "Woman"-themed floor of Beacon Communications includes a beauty parlour next to the conference room.

Opposite page: The kitchen in the "Family" floor doubles as a conference room.

Right: A freestanding ribbon-like divider runs through each floor. Here, on the "Family" floor, the divider is made of wood.

Opposite page: All four clothes brands produced by the company are displayed in the room.
Right: The pressroom of fashion company Gallery de Pop.
Far right: Tsutomu Kurokawa, the designer of the pressroom, also designed the furniture.

The Pressroom of Gallery De Pop Tsutomu Kurokawa designed this pressroom for fashion design company Gallery de Pop in Tokyo, transforming it from its original use as an Italian restaurant. Kurokawa also designed the chairs and furniture.

Gallery De Pop comprises four different fashion "brands", including the Sage de Cret men's clothing line (see also page 152). In the pressroom, all four brands are displayed: men's wardrobe (Sage de Cret), a casual fashion line aimed at 18–25 year olds, a line of "street fashion" clothes, and a lady's simple casual line. Striving to recreate the look of a Western mansion, Kurokawa imported American pine logs for the ceiling.

Located in a quiet area in Shirogane, the office aims to reflect the philosophy and values of the company. Image is crucially important in Japan's huge apparel business, especially at this point in the industry, when big companies and private designers are competing with each other for market share.

GALERIE DE POP CO.,LTD.
SHOW ROOM

Opposite (left) and right: The room features striking LED lights designed by Tsutomu Kurokawa (see page 153).
Below: Tsutomu Kurokawa specially imported pine logs from America to give the room the feeling of a Western mansion.

Far left: The studio and shop of Keiko Matsumoto.
Left (top and bottom): Although she is well known for creating installations, Matsumoto feels that creating accessories from titanium is the best way to express her art.
Opposite page: Glass "bubbles" in the shop feature Matsumoto's work.

Prodottocom This is the shop and studio of Keiko Matsumoto in the Harajuku area of Tokyo. Matsumoto is an artist best known for creating installations. Recently, however, she has been working with titanium, and she now feels that making accessories out of this material is the best way to express her art. Her studio is a perfect illustration of the diminishing gap between designers and consumers in Japan.

Although most consumers purchase goods that are advertised by huge conglomerates, there are some who are wary of advertisements. Matsumoto chose to have her own shop and studio rather than sell her designs to a big company so that she could make contact with these more independently minded shoppers. Of course, having one's own shop and workspace in Harajuku is not economical, but Matsumoto believes that in this era, when consumers are being bombarded with information, it is best to start small and independently and grow through word of mouth.

This is paralleled in the music world, where on the one hand there are musicians who are marketed by large companies who promote their music with a great deal of advertising in the hope of making a hit; on the other, there are independent musicians. It is not rare for

an unknown independent musician to appear at the top of the charts in Japan. The internet also plays a part in the exposure of independent artists, by supercharging a word-of-mouth reputation.

Matsumoto designed the interior of her shop, including the display tables. She has tied her handmade rings to the table with fishing lines, using a nut on the other end of the line to hold them in place. This not only also adds spice to the display but prevents shoplifting. Recently, however, Matsumoto has encountered a more high-tech approach to stealing her designs. Mobile phones that can take pictures are widespread in Japan, and some less scrupulous customers have been using them to photograph her pieces in order to have cheap reproductions made in silver.

From time to time the shop turns into an artistic hang-out – an informal lounge or retreat where Matsumoto welcomes her fellow artists and creatives from the Harajuku area. Matsumoto's space functions as the studio of an independent designer, a shop, and a place for an artistic community.

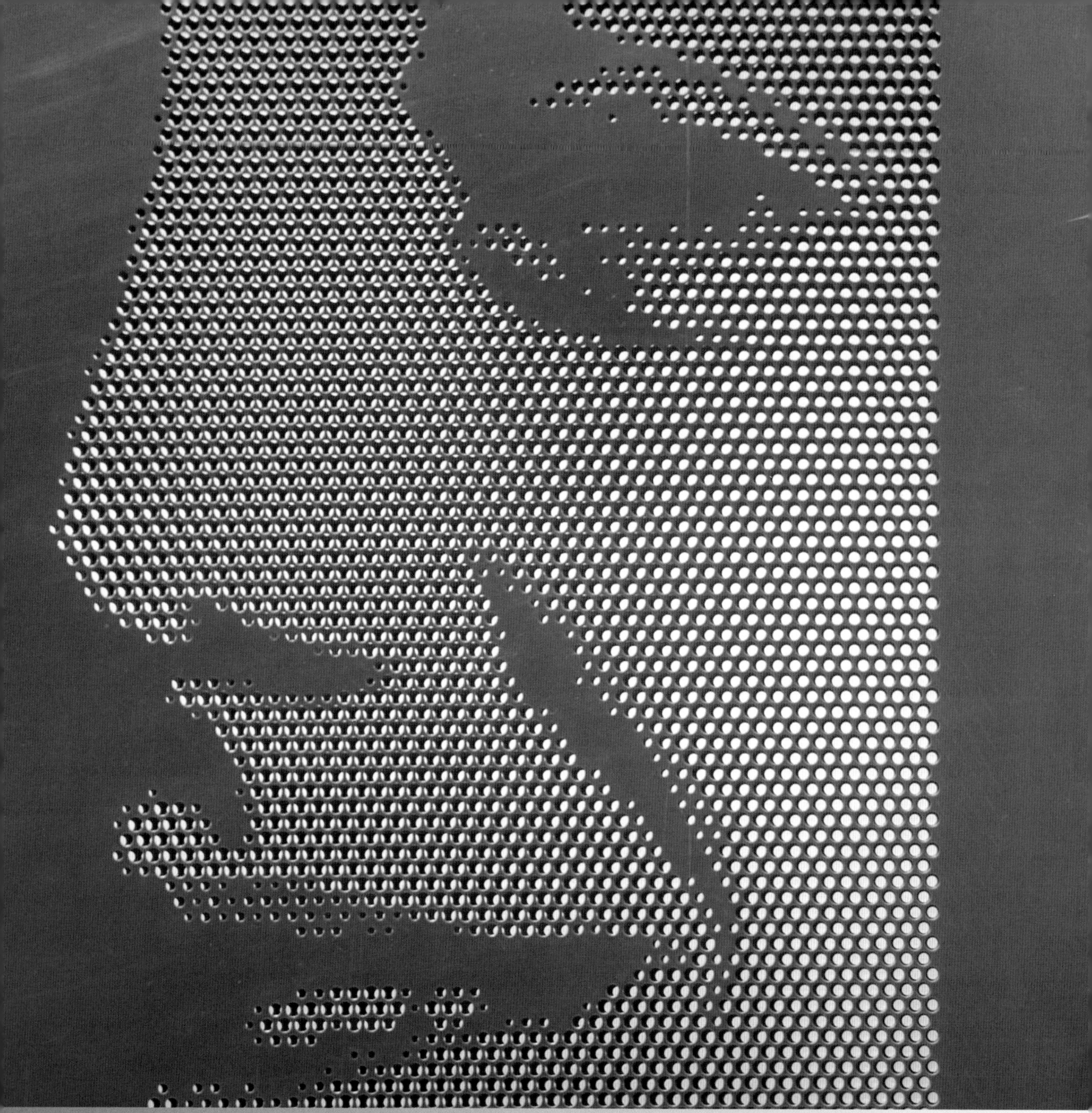

Left: Toshihiko Suzuki at work in his office.
Opposite page: One of Suzuki's punched- metal signs.

Toshihiko Suzuki's Office This is a good example of how a private office can represent a business in a distinctive way, projecting a unique theme and identity. The designer Toshihiko Suzuki has built a reputation by designing buildings and products with aluminium. Suzuki likes working with aluminium because it has both strength and softness. Also, unlike other metals, it warms up when you hold it.

As Suzuki says, "Furniture designed with an architectural idea in mind tends to be functional, but cerebral. Architects tend to regard interiors as something that needs to be filled in; left to their own devices, furniture designed by architects would be equipment-like. I like the idea of functionality, but I try to strike a balance between design and function. I like it when an interior is changeable. Aluminium is a good material in this respect because it is light and easily movable, and the joints can be made with precision. It is the best material to create a balance between furniture (design) and architecture (function)."

The office chairs were jointly designed by Suzuki and a manufacturer. They are part of a product line called Alfuni, a series of rearrangeable furniture using only aluminium pipes. The pipes can be also used for office partitions, depending on their arrangement. Suzuki is aiming to create a complete, co-ordinated office style (called Soho) with this series. Even the stationery on the desk is his design (the Altoo series).

Restaurant Sign To create signs and advertisements, Suzuki "punches" photographs and illustrations into metal plate (not only aluminium, but also steel and stainless steel). Any kind of image can be retouched with a computer and then processed in this way. Punched metal plates can be used to create a wide range of items, from lanterns to fences.

Suzuki used this punched plate method to make a sign for a restaurant (with a flower shop attached) on the corner of a large junction in the city of Yamagata. The owner is a cat lover, and rather than simply create a sign that announced the name of the shop, Suzuki chose to retouch an image of seven cats playing in the woods. As you walk past the sign, there is a moiré effect, which creates the impression that the cats are moving. Not only is the owner of the restaurant delighted with the result, but this purely graphic sign is unsual enough make passers-by stop and look.

Above and opposite page: A sign for a restaurant created from punched metal. A moiré effect makes the cats appear to move as you pass.

Meijo University A place of learning might at first glance seem to be outside the "work" category, but a university is a place where people work together with a purpose, and the new sign of Meijo University offers interesting insights into designing for the world of work. Signs are changing, and so is the perception of design at the university. It used to be the case that careful design was not employed for places of study in Japan – it was not considered necessary for a utilitarian space. But in commemoration of its 75th anniversary, Meijo University in Nagoya decided to build a new school building, and requested graphic designer Masaaki Hiromura to create a sign for it. Hiromura's response was a sign that was, in a sense, made up of the university itself.

Hiromura designed the sign around the idea of memory – not just human memory, but the imagined memory of the university. He took photographs of the old buildings slated for reconstruction, including the library and the canteen. These pictures were a token of how the university has been viewing these buildings and their use over the years. The images were then incorporated into the sign. The motif of the resulting design becomes something far-reaching: a sign marking the passage of time and the freedom to travel through time by using the imagination.

According to Hiromura, as the demand for design increases in more and more fields, the field of design itself is expanding greatly and the boundaries between different kinds of design are blurring. For graphic designers, areas which in the past were considered isolated specialities (advertising, corporate identity, packaging, book design, editorial design, signage, display design, and so on) are no longer so strictly sequestered. They are blending together, opening the entire market for designers.

Hiromura believes that one of the major factors behind this change is the advent of computers and other evolving technologies. Progressively more advanced software programs are popularizing the professional techniques that have been developed among experts in different specialities, making the tools more accessible across disciplines. Information can be collected through the internet from all over the world. The resulting "everyone can be a designer" spirit is promoting a more easygoing attitude in the world of design.

At the same time, designers are being called to deal with increasingly complicated subjects as society itself grows more diverse and complicated. Designing, after all, has the task of conveying information or messages to others with a specific purpose. In a broad sense, design itself is information. According to Hiromura, this is a time to reconsider the essential function of designers.

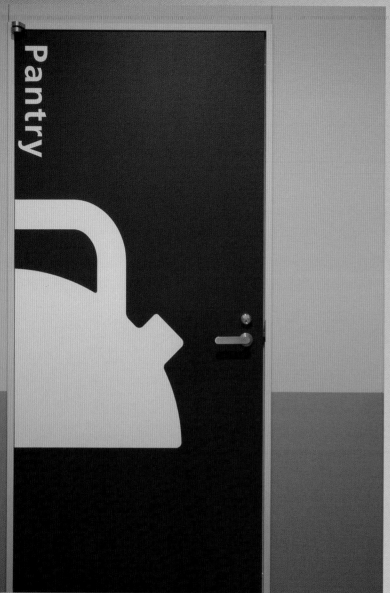

Overleaf and this page: When graphic designer Masaaki Hiromura was commissioned to create signs for new buildings at Meijo University, he decided to incorporate photographs of the buildings that were about to be replaced. His idea was to create a sense of history, of the "memory" of the university.

Previous page, this page, and overleaf:
Views of Tokyo Weld Technical Center, a research facility turned into a company sign by graphic designer Masaaki Hiromura.

Tokyo Weld Technical Center Reaching beyond his work in graphics, Masaaki Hiromura collaborated with architect Riken Yamamoto to design this building in Shizuoka prefecture. Tokyo Weld is a precision machine manufacturer, and this building is the company's research institute. Here, Hiromura uses graphics as an architectural device, running the company name and logo along the walls of an illuminated glass box that serves as entrance and visual focus, connecting the interior and exterior of the building. The building becomes its own sign, in effect, and that sign is always "on", changing with the light and weather. As is evidenced by this project, Hiromura sees an extension of graphic design from simple signage to an integration with the functionality of modern buildings.

Opposite page: Building-as-sign again: Saida Clinic in Kanagawa-ku.
Right: The signage of the Oedo line was one aspect that Ken Yokogawa was not able to change when designing Daimon and Shiodome stations.

Saida Clinic The Saida Clinic building, designed by Guen Bertheau-Suzuki, also plays the role of "sign" for itself. The town's general practitioner works from this building, located in Kanagawa-ku, a small shopping district a few minutes away from the nearest train station. In Japan, as elsewhere, general practitioners hold a special position in society. They are relatively wealthy, and they are depended on by residents of the town. Their clinics need to be hospitable and non-threatening. The doctor at the Saida Clinic also wanted his building to be immediately recognizable in the town. By making the window into the shape of a cross, it became immediately apparent that this was a place to receive medical care. The doctor's consultation room is on the first floor, and behind this cross-shaped window is the private residence of the doctor's family. In the evening, when the family comes home and has dinner, soft light glows through the distinctive "sign" window.

Transportation Design While Tokyo is the birthplace of the latest designs, there is nevertheless a place within the city which has until recently been completely forgotten in terms of design: the train station. Every commuter sees and uses the station daily, but the view of the station has always been seen through a purely functional perspective. Public facilities are typically built with engineering techniques foremost, not design. However, when two new subway lines, the Oedo line and Nanboku line, were being proposed, there was a call for an improved aesthetic as well as an improved function for stations that would be in such frequent use.

Most Japanese subway stations are identical in structure and style, and they blend into the background, taken for granted by their users. They are so similar, in fact, that it is easy to mistake the station you have arrived at if you are not paying close attention to the stops. On the new Oedo line, however, each station has a unique design, making it easy for riders to know exactly where they have arrived – and what to expect there. As Hiromura asserted earlier, design is information.

Daimon station Architect Ken Yokogawa designed two stations on the Oedo line: Daimon station and Shiodome station. Daimon is home to Zojo-ji Temple, which marks the tomb of Tokugawa Shogun. The temple is at the heart of a historic district known as a *monzen-machi* – the equivalent of a cathedral town, where the town developed around a temple at its centre. Daimon is also a growing business hub, with a trade centre and other commercial sites, and the station connects with the Monorail for Haneda airport.

When Yokogawa started to design the station as a public facility, he thought he should take the historical context of Daimon into consideration, as well as the commerce and international travel associated with the station. He decided to find a theme to link these divergent elements, and chose "ink" – a material used extensively in historic temple culture as well as contemporary commercial culture. To focus the theme in a sharp and modern aesthetic, Yokogawa contrasted the silver colour of an aluminium-sheet bench with black Chinese granite, a material metaphor for ink, and Bianco Carrara marble. A contemporary Japanese style is invoked in these carefully considered oppositions.

Above and opposite: Scenes from Daimon station, one of the two stops on the Oedo line designed by Ken Yokogawa. He chose a black-and-white theme at Daimon to evoke the area's past and present.

Above: Architect Ken Yokogawa waits on the platform of Shiodome station. The chair/rest he is using is his own design.
Opposite: The canopy of exit 3 of Roppongi 1 Chome station, designed by Koh Kitayama. His intention was to create a space that would act as a kind of public theatre.

Shiodome station After the inky blackness of Daimon, the next stop on the Oedo line is Shiodome station, which has a sharp white platform. Shiodome has been redeveloped as the third subcentre of the Tokyo metropolis. The largest advertising company in Japan, Dentsu, is located in a new building here. Shiodome has only recently emerged as a strong business area, its high-rise buildings growing up next to the already well-developed hub of Ginza. Yokogawa designed the white Shiodome station to express the innocence and pureness of the rising new centre. The station has the look of a modern art museum, with white floors, white walls, and a white ceiling.

Unfortunately, the designer's freedom was curtailed when it came to the signs for Daimon and Shiodome, as they were required to match the format of those at the other municipal stations. Yokogawa's vision for an ideal station sign is truly an example of the coexistence of design and information: "I would create a sign like a long ribbon printed with the station name, and set up the ribbon from end to end of the platform."

Roppongi 1 Chome Station Exit 3 This station serves one of the main business districts within Roppongi, a district that also houses cultural facilities such as the famous Suntory Concert Hall. Koh Kitayama wanted to create an exit for Roppongi 1 Chome station that was not just a part of an ordinary subway station, but would also function as a kind of stage. He achieved this by building a semicircular stairway assembled simply with basic flat bars to form an amphitheatre.

While the law – and common sense – prevents Kitayama from advertising the space as a concert hall, it is available for street musicians. The audience can gather on the stairs, which become their seats. The stage lighting is provided by the sun that streams through the glass canopy above. Exiting the station from down on the platform, passengers feel as if they are stepping up into a huge greenhouse.

Kitayama shares his strategy of how he relates to the city as an architect: "Urban space systematically places pressure on people much more than any other kind of space does. The city as we experience it now is dominated by capitalism. All urban problems are either

political or are related to the fact that the city is controlled by the economy. People tend to ignore these problems since the idea of the city itself is a huge fiction. We need to change the system of society to release people from the idea of 'city'. I am thinking of how architects could help in this. We should experiment with new ways to create vacant space in the city, leaving behind the overwhelming system defined by capitalism. By creating spaces, one obtains a release from the system. When many of these spaces are combined into a network, they create a new city experience, which would promote a new lifestyle."

Iidabashi station Makoto Shin Watanabe designed Iidabashi station to incorporate a long "creeper" made from green pipes running from the ceiling on the platform level (floor B6) up five flights (to floor B1). "Underground is strictly the territory of engineering," says Watanabe. "In the engineering world, they are satisfied with the ceiling if it is high enough for people to walk under without hitting their heads. They think space without specific purpose is a waste."

Watanabe tried to challenge these typical expectations and restrictions in his station design. When he was told that the architect was not expected to do much with the station beyond designing the colour of the tiles, he responded by questioning why the station had to be lined with tiles at all. He moved from that starting point to create new rules for his station. The most basic was that all the framed structures in the station were to be exposed as long as they did not leak. By moving all of the ducts and pipes out from their hiding place behind the typical dropped ceiling, the ceiling could be higher.

It is difficult to create a new precedent in Japan, and it was a struggle to persuade the powers that be to accept Watanabe's idea of leaving such structures exposed. He did eventually persuade them that it was important to show off the engineering to the commuters. Everyone has got his or her own "work" space, and now the commuters were to be shown the "work" space of the engineers. What could be a better urban plan?

Clockwise from top left: Beacon Communications,

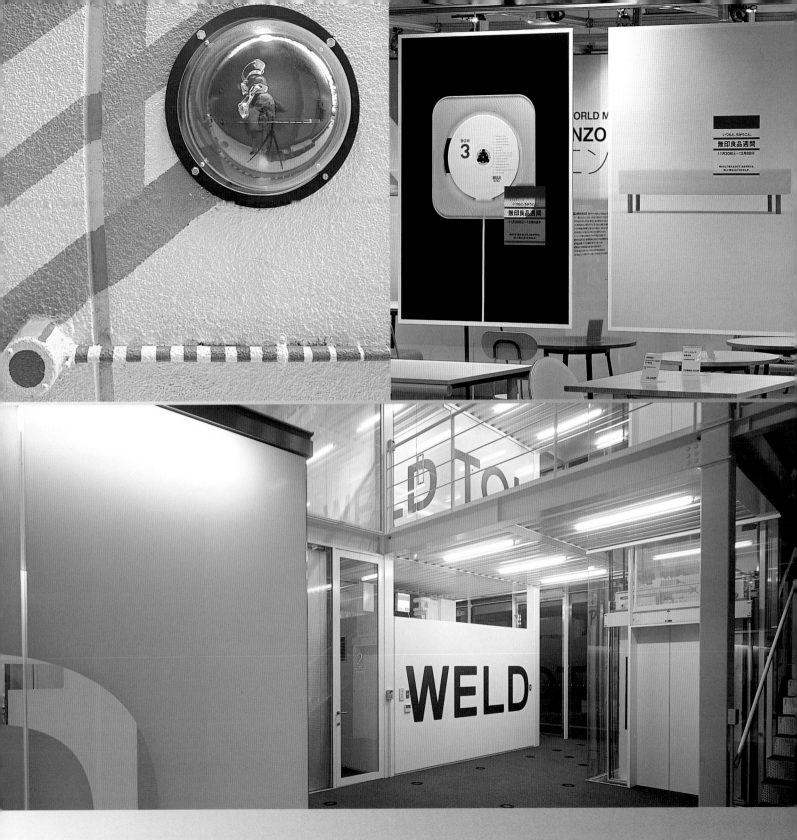

Prodottocom, Muji, Tokyo Weld, Muji, Bloomberg ICE.

こちらまで、
ご返却ください。

Opposite page: The Muji store at Yurakucho. Ironically, the success of Muji's "no brand" approach to design has made it an extremely successful brand in itself.
Right: A temporary art installation at the store.
Overleaf: Muji offers its own make of glasses in Japan. Typically, they offer good design at a reasonable price.

Muji (Mujirushi Ryohin) "There is no right answer to the question 'What is the best product?'" This is the message Muji has been sending for over twenty years, apparently very successfully. Muji is a chain with 267 shops in Japan, and 26 shops overseas, including locations in the UK, France, and Hong Kong. Muji's debut in the 1980s was front-page news.

The concept behind the shop was to eliminate such a thing as a "brand name", as the name Muji itself implies (Mujirushi means "no-brand", and Ryohin means "good product"). Ironically, people began to recognize Muji as the "No-brand brand". These days, Muji continues its generic crusade, deciding not to publicize the name of the designer on the products that the chain offers, even when the designers are some of Japan's most prominent. Instead, Muji displays a product and lets the consumer see it for themselves, and make their own decision about the item's quality.

A store like Muji that doesn't advertise a name acts as a new kind of "work" space for designers; a showcase to present themselves through their work, not their reputation. Some of the offerings at Muji are only picked up by the shops after they have sold well in test trials on the internet. The cordless light (shown opposite) is one such product. The commodities at Muji are not only for ordinary people; the stores also stock goods for professionals, such as DIY materials and kitchen tools.

WORK

Above: Mrs Hamano's "perfect kitchen" in the Omni Quarter house, created for the iconoclastic designer Yasuhiro Hamano by Koh Kitayama.
Opposite page: Hamano's audiovisual room.
Overleaf: Living/office space in the Omni Quarter house.

When the Japanese economy was booming, style and fashion tended to be dictated from the top down. New products and designs were developed and unveiled by designers and manufacturers, and the public went along with whatever was the new thing. But these days, there's a sense that people want to be able to determine what surrounds them, especially in their time off. In Japan's less active economy, the principle of rest has greater resonance.

When people choose products and spaces for which they have real affection, a feeling of serenity of restfulness, can be the result. New technology has given us an overflow of information. We must learn to filter that information and choose what is really important to us. These choices help us trim away the materialistic excess and carve out something – or some time – that has real value.

Omni Quarter Although Japanese design is presently in this anti-conceptual phase, there is one celebrated designer who bucks the trend – the iconoclastic Yasuhiro Hamano. Omni Quarter is Yasuhiro Hamano's house and it serves many functions for him. In it, he can work, do business, entertain, rest, or spend time with his family.

The glass box structure, designed by Koh Kitayama, is remarkable. It consists of an art gallery and an atelier on the basement floor, rentable space for shops on the first and second floors, some private living quarters also on the second floor, and a huge living space that can be used for parties on the third floor.

When he started the assignment, Kitayama decided to employ a rigid-frame reinforced concrete structure to subdivide the space. Hamano required an extraordinarily flexible space, one that could accommodate the fluctuations of both family and professional life. Since there were going to be commercial tenants on the lower floors and their needs were not yet known, Kitayama had to create a structure that favoured possibility over unity – a flexible structural skeleton that could be redesigned as the owner saw fit. Hamano arrived at this approach by picturing the building as a flow of motion, rather than merely as an inert object.

In effect, this house has two layers of skin. The outer skin, made of glass, blocks the wind and rain but lets in sunlight. The inner skin is a screen which shades the indoors from the sun and creates a sense of privacy.

Kitayama ingeniously incorporated large appliances (a dehumidifier, the heating system) and ventilation shafts into his overall design. Mrs Hamano called upon this skill when it came to design her perfect kitchen. The kitchen has an open style, and enough workspace to entertain comfortably. Kitayama's creativity overcame logistical problems that are inherent in many kitchens. His custom-designed shelves hold long-stemmed wine glasses, and his drawers hold small plates, for example, providing easy access to items that often get shuffled to the back of deep shelves.

That ubiquitous Japanese kitchen item the rice cooker also has its own custom-made storage space. Mrs Hamano feels that items that are reminders of daily family life, even the refrigerator, are not suitable for public view. It is not just that they are "private" items; she also feels that the poor external design of Japanese household electrical appliances makes them unfit for "public" display. Kitayama has kept them hidden, and the kitchen meets Mrs Hamano's exacting standards.

Hamano had always planned to move to the city when he reached a certain age, and it is fitting that he came to the Aoyama district, where Tokyo's cutting-edge designs are born. He speaks about his building with obvious affection. For him, every element of the structure has its own aesthetic and functional purpose. He even describes the stairs as bringing a "rough warmth to our daily life".

Opposite page: Living/office space in Omni Quarter.

Below: Hamano's audiovisual room again. This time it has been sectioned off from the living area to create an cosy, intimate environment.

Hamano says, "I'm frequently asked what my speciality is. But I don't want to be defined by one hackneyed title. My work has its own nature. It is neither 'play' nor 'work'. It doesn't care if it is daytime or nighttime, a weekday or a holiday. It is just my life and my lifestyle."

Hamano was born in 1941. Although he is now labelled a conceptualist, he himself had a role in the present turn away from conceptualism. Many years ago, it was Hamano who urged the Japanese people to realize the existence of freedom; it was he who first proposed the idea that one's lifestyle should reflect one's reason for being.

The gallery in the underground level of Omni Quarter has played host a lighting exhibition by Tsutomu Kurokawa (pages 94–5) among others, and on the ground-floor level is the boutique of fashion designer Chisato Tsumori. Its interior was created by Hisae Igarashi (pages 10–11 and 78).

Hamano says that he plans to close the gallery, however. "At one time, there were very few galleries in Omotesando Street regardless of its reputation as one of the most fashionable areas in Tokyo and the heart of the new culture. But my gallery has served its purpose, and it has paved the way for many other galleries to open. It has carried out its duty well."

Vingt cinq ans Style1

Opposite page: The reception area of La Une. Its muted, restful appearance is designed to cleanse shoppers' palates to enhance their appreciation of the items in the shop.
Right: A typical display in the shop. Diverse pieces of furniture and accessories have been brought together to create a coordinated whole.

La Une When customers go from store to store purchasing home furnishings, it can be difficult for them to keep a complete picture in mind. La Une, based on a concept by Yasuhiro Hamano, is a shop that presents items in a coordinated fashion to guide the customer towards a coherent vision.

La Une doesn't necessarily cater to current trends. For example, Italian furniture is currently popular in Japan, and customers tend to look for Italian brand names. But La Une carries products that their coordinators have chosen to fit together and exemplify a certain lifestyle — some designed by Japanese designers, some by foreign designers; furniture with Japanese motifs, furniture without any motifs at all. A parallel may be found in the Japanese aquarium. Fish used to be grouped by family or habitat, but it is now more popular to group many kinds of fish in one large tank, to "reproduce the sea". To look at a large aquarium and feel a diverse presence of

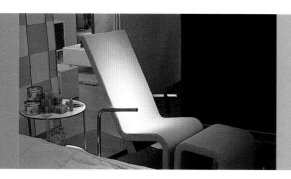

Left: An unsually streamlined massage chair at La Une.
Opposite page: A co-ordinated suite from the "lovely living" section of La Une, aimed at married couples.
Overleaf: Another suite at La Une.

fish is far more entertaining than seeing a segregated selection in a small tank, even though it may be easier to learn the proper names and habitat of each fish. Similarly, La Une aims for a totality of experience and lifestyle, rather than concentrating on name brands.

Yoshihiro Kato, a commercial architect based in Nagoya, designed the shop's bold front entrance. As customers pass through the sliding front door, they feel as if they are entering a different world. Ginza is an important centre of commerce and culture (land here is the most expensive in all Japan). Kato wanted to erase the city's frenetic colours and sounds from customers' minds before they viewed the work of world-class designers. This recalls the beginning of the traditional Japanese tea ceremony. Before entering the tearoom, guests need to clear their minds by walking along the little garden path that leads to its entrance.

There is one section of La Une that is completely dedicated to newly married couples: "Lovely Living". Here one can find a remarkable red sofa designed by Toshihiko Sakai. "Attachment is a key word for me," Sakai says. "I want people to feel attached to my designs. If they are attached to a product, then they will keep it for a long time. Let's say the product lasts ten years maximum. If people love the product, they will maintain it well and keep it as long as they can, and there is less waste in the world … I'd like to see the development of 'long-life' products in home furnishing." This is reminiscent of the ideas of Louis Poulsen, the famous Danish lighting designer. The main theme of Danish design is also attachment. Perhaps because they are not a rich country, they recognize the need to love what they have and make it last longer. Japan is starting to recognize the value behind this idea.

The current popularity of Italian furniture notwithstanding, if you would like to purchase items that fit together and create a real Japanese lifestyle, La Une is the shop to visit.

Body Relax Fuu There are those who would say that Japan's massage craze has come and gone. But it hasn't really gone away; there are many people who have become dedicated devotees. It's just that the cost and inconvenience of having a massage had become prohibitive: typically, one needed to book in advance, and the session would cost approximately 6,000 yen, last over an hour, and be at an inconvenient location. The massage business is now in the process of refashioning itself, however, using the fast food industry as a model. Consumers can now choose the time, place, type of massage, and price range – for example, one can receive a massage for ten minutes costing 1,000 yen, or get a 30-minute reflexology treatment for 2,500 yen. And the salons are becoming plentiful and conveniently located, sometimes right in front of the train station.

As the massage clientele gets younger, and young women (and men) are starting to reap the benefits of a treatment formerly thought to be for the older generation, the salons themselves are becoming more fashionable. After consulting with his friend, designer Yudai Tachikawa, the owner of Body Relax Fuu decided to entrust the whole design of the shop to Hisae Igarashi.

"I investigated this space much more carefully than any other place I've designed," says Igarashi. Her efforts paid off, and the salon now looks more spacious than it actually is. Light falls through the ceiling, creating an illusion of height – especially important because of the salon's drop ceiling, which could give an impression of compressed space. Igarashi successfully relieved that potential pressure by creating flow. "What I always put stress on when I produce shops is to create a open place where you feel that the air flows freely. Even a small change such as adding a slight curve to the entrance can help the air come inside and let it flow." Igarashi also designed the massage chairs themselves, bringing fashionability and attractiveness to a particularly egregious example of the poor product design discussed earlier.

Star Garden This is a three-floor total beauty "experience". On the ground floor there is the reception area, beauty goods shop, nail care salon, and private make-up room. The first floor, dedicated to relaxation and body care, consists of a body massage room, an aromatherapy treatment room, and a dental care room. The top floor is a hair salon.

The location is convenient, a pleasant, quiet area near the downtown Shibuya section of Tokyo. Akihito Fumita, the designer, aimed to provide a space that was relaxing for customers and where beauticians could move around freely. His movable workstations carry the beauty equipment and hide all unsightly electric cords. He used his favourite material, a milky coloured acrylic board, for the partitions. The boards reflect light softly and help to induce a sense of relaxation.

M Premier This boutique, located in the Mitsukoshi department store (at a busy intersection in Ginza), has become popular among women through its design, which makes shopping more enjoyable and therefore more relaxing. The boutique is dedicated to bringing out the elegance in real, modern women; its dresses are generally simple but up to the minute.

Fumita used an artificial marble called Cori Light for the back wall of the show window. Without any retouching, the wall allows some light to pass through; but by shaving the material, he was able to change the shade of the light. Combined with stainless steel and glass, the white light coming through the Cori Light material creates a singular impression.

Art Rush At first glance, you would never guess that this is a hair salon. The designer Takahiro Maeda collaborated with the owner to design a salon that emphasized certain key ideas. They wanted a space with an enclosed feeling and no bright lights (spotlights were used). A space with curved lines. A space that had a classically modern style, not too simple, and which borrowed from nature. A space with a sense of surprise. Ultimately, they created a space that makes you feel as protected as if you were inside a cocoon.

Generally, hair salons are bright, open, and inviting – not just to please the customer, but to make the place attractive to those looking in from the outside. The designers of Art Rush decided to make their salon into a relaxing retreat, a place where the customer does not have to be exposed to strangers passing by.

An air purification system, with negative ion-producing ability, was installed. This has the effect not only of purifying the air, but also of promoting the general well-being of the customer. Art Rush is relaxing and very "pop", a hair salon for women who want to unwind inside a cocoon in Aoyama.

Opposite page far left: The facial treatment room at Star Garden.
Opposite page left: The hair salon at Star Garden, featuring the special movable workstations to carry the beauty equipment (left).
Below: The diffused white light at M Premier boutique comes from the use of a translucent artifical marble.
Overleaf: Art Rush hair salon.

Myougei This 100-year-old house in the Ukyo district of Kyoto was converted into a gallery after the owner decided that he had had enough of the region's severely cold winters. Miyadaiku, a temple-building carpenter and the present owner's ancestor, built this house, and it does indeed look like a temple. It is considerably larger than other Machiya style (traditional Japanese town house) homes. Old and new are linked in this area: nearby is a Myoshin-ji temple, also built by Miyadaiku. An old iron pot exhibited there was in use until recently.

Katsu Umebayashi of the FOBA architectural firm was in charge of the remodelling of Myougei. While respecting the great skill with which it was built, Umebayashi added a touch of modernity to this historic house. The staircase leading to the upper floor uses a passive light wall, for example. The modern wall promotes the connection between past and present, calling attention to the passage of time experienced by the house. This gallery is an excellent space for the exhibition of both modern and classical artwork. Many young avant-garde artists visit and show their work here.

Mai Michimasa Kawaguchi has a reputation as an architect who creates strong, modern Japanese designs that are grounded in a thorough knowledge of traditional Japanese architecture. "The most popular style in Japanese traditional building is the *sukiya* style. In my estimation, this style matured in the 1970s and it died in the bubble era. By the 1970s, proponents of the *sukiya* style – which can be

described as a style of simplification, the elimination of unnecessary decoration – had run out of new ideas, and ended up turning out the same things over and over again. Then in the bubble era the style began to be ignored and architects started to decorate in earnest."

Kawaguchi has pioneered a new Japanese style, one that fits into current lifestyles and uses modern materials. At one time, a "Japanese-style" house had by definition to be made of wood. Kawaguchi has succeeded in creating a Japanese-style gallery, Mai, with a mixture of traditional and modern materials. His *juraku-kabe* (a wall first used in the 16th-century Azuchi Momoyama era) covers a concrete structure. Kawaguchi plastered the wall with a fine layer of earth, and when was is dry, covered it with the characteristically fine-grained yellowish soil (*juraku*). He repeated this process several times to recreate the traditional *juraku-kabe*.

"People say that a traditional Japanese residence, like a human being, has five senses," Kawaguchi states. We treasure a space where we feel that those senses are not being compromised. I use concrete in the gallery because it is inevitable and right to pair it with new music and images. But I also wanted to use the traditional wall to bring in a pleasant sense of tradition." Mai mainly displays works of artists discovered by the owner himself. It is located in Iidabashi; families often come here to relax, and local residents often drop by when they are out for a stroll.

Gallery Tenshinan Eiichi Nomura, the president of a computer company, has converted his living room into a gallery. Gallery Tenshinan is located in a residential area in Itabashi, one station stop away from Ikebukuro. Nomura wanted the space to be a salon, a place where young artists or chefs and other artisans could gather and talk about art.

Takeshi Nagasaki designed a garden for the roof of the gallery, called Ima no Niwa (*ima* means modern; *niwa* means garden). Nagasaki is a gardener by profession; he also works as a writer. He created modern *tobiishi* (stepping stones) from glass and bronze and modelled

on bamboo, one of the typical plants found in a traditional Japanese garden. Using an essential technique of Japanese gardening called *shakkei* (in which part of a distant landscape is "captured" and brought into the garden) Nagasaki harmonized the garden with a borrowed view of Ikebukuro.

The glass bamboo is also built into a table in the gallery itself, creating an afterimage of the garden. Mr Nomura's salons encourage the young artists to appreciate the elemental beauty of the garden and the gallery. Nagasaki also created glass stepping stones with inlaid lights. They are called *sho-lo* (a pun expressing the narrow line between art and products).

There is also an object at the gallery called a *to-lo*, a framed woodblock print that can be used as a lantern. Although *to-lo* actually means garden lantern, it does not function as a lantern in this setting, because there is no lighting device inside it. Nagasaki says, "If I put the light inside it, it becomes a product with a clear purpose. I wanted to leave that sense of purpose open, to be 'filled in' by the observer or by the garden itself."

Clockwise from top left: The roof garden at Gallery Tenshinan,

Close-up of *tobiishi* at Gallery Tenshinan, *to-lo* lights, sashimi, *to-lo* light.

Hotaru Between Back to the modern age. Most people born after the war would think of Hotaru Between as a modern tea room. Actually it is modelled on a type of traditional but Westernized tea ceremony room called *ryurei-shiki*. At the beginning of the Meji era (1868–1912), Gengen Sai, the master of the Japanese tea ceremony at that time, invented this new style of tea ceremony for foreigners that used chairs and tables instead of requiring participants to sit on a tatami mat.

Masayuki Kurokawa, the creator of Hotaru Between, is mostly known for his product design, but he thinks architecturally. Kurokawa ingeniously uses a well-known Japanese architectural element, the *akari-shoji* or translucent paper screen, to create furniture. (*Akari-shoji* is used in Japanese houses for partitions and in windows.) Kurokawa's transformed furniture, called *ryurei*, was on display in New York in 2002 at "The New Way of Tea" exhibition, held at The Japan Society.

Kurokawa describes this work as *sukiya* style turned inside out. Put another way, he turns architecture inside out to create furniture. "Architecture creates a space for objects to exist within, whereas objects influence the space surrounding them. Looked at as an object, a pillar influences its surrounding space. But when several pillars are arranged in a circle, the space becomes focused on the area created within the false circular wall circumscribed by the pillars."

Kaze Masayuki Kurokawa's electric light is another example of his theory of turning architecture inside out to create furniture. Two oval polypropylene sheets are zipped together to create the light, calling to mind once again the translucent *akari-shoji* that typically would be used to allow sunlight into a Japanese *sukiya*-style house. Here, however, the *akari-shoji* themselves become the light source. Kurokawa named the lamp *kaze* (meaning wind). Even the wind is an object of beauty for the Japanese, another element called to stimulate each of the five senses.

It is not uncommon for architects and interior designers to design their own, original products. For them, product design is part of a larger effort to create a whole coordinated space. Generally, their product design is informed by architectural thinking and tends to be sophisticated and innovative. This is not surprising since architects and interior designers are on the cutting edge when it comes to the exploration and utilization of new materials.

Cinderella Clock Designed by architect Guen Bertheau-Suzuki, this clock consists of 100% recycled material, fashioned from the paper that comes from milk cartons. The Cinderella Clock is sold mainly through the internet. Its name derives from Suzuki's belief that its design "can be perfect only twice a day, at midnight and noon".

Tango Chest Designed by Hisae Igarashi. This is a simple chest, made from maple, without handles or metal fixtures of any kind. Its smooth curve creates a shadow that can create a subtle complexity depending on where the chest is placed.

Richard Scott Isaac This experimental designer has lived and worked in Tokyo for nine years, creating collages from the technological detritus of Japan's consumer products. Video recorders, computer chips, and abandoned hard drives are all recycled through his imagination in works that are both a little cynical and provocative to the typical Japanese consumer's love of the new.

His workshop is partly a warehouse of bins, with collections of disassembled home and office appliances. "Individually, they are no longer identifiable with their original machine," he says, "and they find themselves to be raw material once again. My enjoyment is bringing life and a new sense to the materials I collect." Isaac emphasizes that Tokyo rather than Japan as a whole is a good inspiration for design and art, because of its constant change. "You don't get comfortable in an old street; instead you get into a forever-changing environment. Trend, change, and experimentation is what Tokyo is about. It's a life's work and very difficult to leave, especially if you can't resist challenges."

Artists such as Isaac help to make Japanese product design borderless by inverting the design – even subverting it – for the young Tokyo market. There is an element of industrial nostalgia here that is beginning to appear in other parts of the city, such as in Takashi Sugimoto's Shunkan mall in Shinjuku, where encrusted televison sets and computers line the walkways like excavations into earlier strata. The Japanese are beginning to go back in time.

Lenorat Designed by Tsutomu Kurokawa, this beautiful flower vase is illuminated by LEDs (Light Emitting Diodes). The vase takes full advantage of one of LED's greatest assets – they don't generate heat. Kurokawa also created the Maty LED light which he has used to

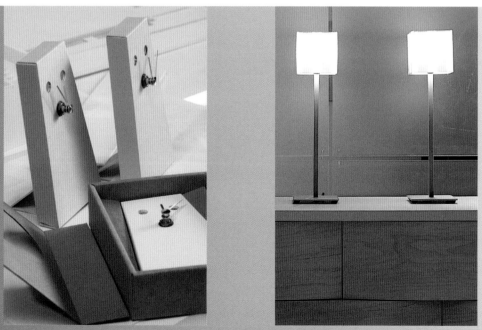

Far left: Guen Beatheau-Suzuki's Cinderella Clock.
Left: Tango Chest by Hisae Igarashi (detail).
Opposite page: Richard Scott Issac's studio.
Overleaf: Lenorat flower vase lights by Tsutomu Kurokawa. The chairs and tables were also designed by Kurokawa.

illustrate interiors in two of his projects discussed in this book: the pressroom of the Gallery De Pop (see page 32) and Sage De Cret boutique (see page 152).

The Terrace This building, constructed right next to a park, serves architect Ken Yokogawa as a space in which he can work, rest, and, play. A café/restaurant is on the ground floor; a shop that sells lights and chairs designed by Yokogawa is on the second floor; his office is on the third floor; and his hobby room is on the fourth floor.

Yokokawa's office used to be located in Azabu, one of the most fashionable areas in Tokyo. But he decided to move here after he found out that the land next to the park was vacant: "It is very luxurious to own a building next to a park. People need to consider their house as not only a place for shelter and dwelling, but also a place from which one can establish a good relationship with the surrounding environment." The new spaciousness allows him to surround himself not only with work-related items, but also with things that relate to his hobbies.

The building was constructed using a relatively new and unknown method called Hybrid RC. Unlike the traditional *kumiishi-zukuri*, the ancient Japanese construction method, which used stones, bricks, and soil for materials; the Hybrid RC method calls for reinforced-concrete and steel skeletons, contemporary materials for longevity and flexibility.

Opposite page: The roof of Plastic House, a flexible living and working space designed for a photographer by Kengo Kuma.
Right: A front view of Plastic House. The ground floor is the photographer's studio and the first floor is the office and living space.

Plastic House For many years, people in Japan blindly followed the so-called "LDK myth". LDK, an abbreviation for living room, dining room, and kitchen, is used to describe the basic plan of a house. For example, 2LDK means that the house consists of two bedrooms, a living room, dining room, and kitchen. People used to believe that the more rooms a house had, the better – regardless of the actual size of each room. But with changes in Japanese lifestyle, people started to think differently.

All the elements of work, rest, and play are packed into this photographer's house. The shooting studio on the ground floor can be converted into a party space. Or, if the open-styled kitchen is used, the space can be used for cooking demonstrations. With *tatami* mats on the floor, the space becomes a tea ceremony room, taking advantage of the green space outside that was specifically created for *nodate* (the open-air tea ceremony).

The floor is covered with FRP (polycarbonate). FRP is generally not used in the decoration of a house, but the architect, Kengo Kuma, was fond of its milky greenish colour with its resemblance to bamboo. It is his way of conveying "Edo" (the old name of Tokyo), and proves the point that plastic can be used to express traditional Japanese style and values. Kuma likes to surprise people with his choice of materials. He feels that modern architecture is uncomfortably bound by political correctness, and that architects today tend to choose easy and safe materials to match their surroundings, such as bamboo, wood, stone, and paper.

Plastic house is located in one of the quiet, agreeable residential areas in Tokyo, only 30 minutes away from Shibuya at the centre of the city. Many of the neighbours have deep roots in the area, and there is a nice balance of old and new styles. Kuma's inclination to use new materials tastefully is a style that suits the neighbourhood well.

The photographer's bedroom and office space are on the second floor of the house. The rooftop can also be used as an open party space. All eyesores (hot water heater, etc) are hidden in nooks and crannies that are, again, treated with FRP (giving the effect of bamboo groves). The basement has been converted into a separate apartment, and is occupied by the owner's mother, an antique collector who has opened her own gallery there.

Left and opposite page: NT House, an open-plan living space designed to meet the needs of the new "non-nuclear" family.

The owner wanted to live in a house that still retains the functionality of the traditional Japanese house: "I wanted to live in a space not with decorative beauty, but with simple beauty." And of course, as a photographer, the effect of light and shadow is important to him.

Plastic house recalls a characteristic attributed to native Tokyo-ites: *isagiyosa*, meaning a graceful attitude that doesn't harp upon any one thing in particular. This word is a good description of Kuma's design, a design that removes as much decoration as possible, and results in a refreshing environment.

NT House As lifestyles changed in Japan, people started to move away from the LDK myth and rethink the layout of their homes. NT House is a collaborative work by Makoto Watanabe and Yoko Kinoshita; it can be described as two one-story houses on top of each other.

The occupants of NT house are a family with two working parents and two children. Superficially, one could say that this is a typical "nuclear family", but as lifestyles change, that term is becoming obsolete. The term "non-nuclear family" is on the rise in Japan, and the definition is expanding. It can be used to refer to not only an extended family, but also bachelors, a single-parent family, and complex families reconstituted by divorce and remarriage. Architect Kinoshita says that house planning based on the ideal nuclear family make-up is now outdated.

How does change within Japanese society towards an increasingly non-nuclear family affect modern architecture? For one thing, children are spending more time by themselves, since their parents both work. Equally, an increased interest in security tends to make parents want to keep their children indoors, protected by security systems, and to shut out the outside world.

Below: The work space of NT House.
Opposite page: The kitchen area of
NT House, joined onto the dining area to
encourage family members to help with
food preparation.

This leads to two tendencies: as outward growth is limited (going outside), upward growth is encouraged (building more levels). And as parents feel that they have less time to spend with their family, there is an attempt to compensate by building more common areas (dining rooms and libraries, for example) that promote family togetherness.

Kinoshita and Watanabe have responded to these social changes by creating a system called CPS to design living spaces. The "C" is an abbreviation of common areas, "S" stands for satellites (meaning private rooms), and the "P" denotes passageways that link "C" to "S".

On the ground floor of NT house there is a library and a dining room, and there are steps leading from one to the other. These rooms serve as a common space for the family (although the library can be used as a private study if it is needed as such). Typically in a Japanese house, the dining room and kitchen are separate, but in this house they share one large area, encouraging each family member who enters the space to help with food preparation.

Below: Skip house. Its inward-looking
design reflects the increasing desire for
privacy and security in Japan.
Opposite page: Two views of the
headquarters of the FOBA architecture
firm, creators of the Skip house.

Skip House This Kyoto house has been under construction for five years by the FOBA firm – founded and run by Katsu Umebashi. Since the owner had another residence, FOBA could focus on completing their elaborate design and not worry about a stringent time limit.

Like NT House, this house is also a reflection of the changes within Japanese society. The roof can be used not only for party space, but also as a garden terrace. While this garden is not visible from the street, it does allow the family to enjoy a view. The desire for privacy and concerns about security have led to an opening-up of interior space.

The kitchen and the bathroom are on the ground floor of Skip House. The bathroom is housed inside a pillar. On the mezzanine floor, there is an orange-coloured *tatami* room, which one enters through a subtly designed, curvilinear living room.

The brightness of the orange colour coming through the *shoji* screen is a suprising sight, almost like seeing a glowing lantern outside. This brings to mind the theory of Masayuki Kurokawa about of the relationship between furniture (particularly screens) and architecture (see page 90). The *tatami* room itself plays the part of a lantern, setting off and contrasting the interior space and the garden.

Above: The *tatami* room in Skip
House with its unusual orange colour.
Right: The rooftop of Skip House, which
acts as a secluded garden terrace and
party space.
Opposite page: The living room of Skip
House. The bathroom is located inside
the white pillar on the left.

On the third floor, all the rooms are connected and accessible to each other through the garden, which functions as the common space in the house. The nature of the corridor, therefore, may also be evolving as Japanese society changes.

The bathroom-in-a-pillar is one of several deliberate concealments built into the design, making the residence a modern version of a *karakuri* house. *Karakuri*, referring to something constructed with tricks, employs secretiveness and misdirection, a style favoured by *ninja* in the Edo period. Here it is used more playfully, to create a sense of hidden spaces and surprise. Other instances of this in the house are a narrow concealed stairway leading to an upper suite of rooms, and the many separate access routes to the roof gardens.

Tokyo Tower Not so long ago, a night view was something you had to go outside to enjoy; it was part of nature. But when critics started to tout and rank out-of-the-way spots for enjoying excellent night views, people started to regard them in a new light. The owners of restaurants and skyscraper bars, who used to regard happening to have a good view as a kind of optional extra, are now attempting to capitalize on the "night view phenomenon".

The restaurants and bars use the Japanese gardening technique of *shakkei* to help to attract customers. As was mentioned earlier (see page 87), *shakkei* is a technique of designing a better view from the garden by capturing, framing, and masking a distant vista. Perhaps the best example of this in action is the Tokyo Tower.

When this world-famous landmark made its debut in 1958, its primary attraction was its height (333 metres; 109 feet). As the city's airspace started to fill with other high-rise buildings, however, the Tokyo Tower lost its attraction and people's interest declined. But architect Koh Kitayama has resurrected the Tokyo Tower, turning it into one of the hottest dating spots in the 21st century.

Kitayama's main gambit was the Observation Museum, making Tokyo Tower into a gallery that displays Tokyo's night view more beautifully than anywhere else. He added sci-fi effects to the museum, allowing visitors to imagine the future and to project themselves into space. He covered the floors with a non-slip, tempered glass, and used glass as material for walls and pillars, creating a translucent effect.

The city becomes reversible in a sense. While you are unable to notice how the city looks up close when you're living in it, there is nevertheless a way you can see the view from outside — from above. This way you can escape from Tokyo while actually staying inside the city. Here, freedom, a recurring theme in contemporary Japanese design, is an expansion of both the horizontal and the vertical planes.

Opposite and below: The viewing gallery
of the Tokyo Tower, turned into the
Observation Museum by architect
Koh Kitayama.

REST

It used to be hard work to find an empty taxi cruising the streets late at night in Japan. They would all be filled with businessmen coming home from a very long day's work. Well, now that the economy has slowed down, it's easier to find a taxi at night. Less work means less overtime, and businessmen aren't missing their last train home anymore. With work less central to people's lives, there is an increased interest in the enjoyment of leisure. Japanese people are trying to figure out how to have fun within a limited budget and timeframe.

One solution has been the creation of *makunouchi-bento* spaces – places where you can satisfy all your leisure needs at once. *Makunouchi-bento* is a type of lunch box that contains small portions of various dishes (Japanese, Western, and Chinese-style rice, fish, meat, fried vegetables, salad, pickles) beautifully served in little compartments. These *bento*-type restaurants or boutiques tend to push the boundaries of traditional Japanese style (*Wa*) by including elements of surprise. The goal is to delight the customer; there's something of the amusement park in these modernized, Japanese settings.

Souen According to restauranteur Yasuhiro Harada, "Japan is now in a restaurant bubble." It is boomtime in the catering industry, with restaurants constantly opening and closing. Because it is taken for granted that the food will be good (standards are consistently high in Japan because of consumer expectations) and the price reasonable, the success or failure of a restaurant can depend on the quality of the interior design and theme. The expectation is not simply that the design will be good, but that it will have an element of surprise.

Interior designer Yoshiyuki Morii realized Harada's ideas to create Souen, a restaurant located in Aoyama on Route 246, one of the busiest and most popular areas in Tokyo. The device is that while the restaurant is underground, diners are given a special kind of garden view, and can enjoy Japanese-style food in a relaxed atmosphere. An immediate attraction is that one can have a meal with a 5,000-yen (£30) budget in an expensive area of town in a strikingly designed space – expensive, perhaps, by the standards of most Western cities, but in Tokyo very reasonable indeed. Harada's marketing strategy has been to use word of mouth: "The restaurant is unusual enough that people will feel they have to see and check for themselves."

Harada chose the name "Souen" to play on different meanings in *kanji* (the Japanese version of Chinese characters), although he deliberately avoided using the *kanji* itself. His primary intention was to refer to the meanings *sou* (layers of garden) and *en*, which signifies enclosed land. But the sound of those *kanji* syllables have other meanings as well, like English homonyms. The syllable *sou* (represented by different characters), can also mean to create or to imagine; the *en* sound, spelled differently, can mean direction or party. So the name of the restaurant itself, according to Harada, invites the guest to play imaginatively, using their mind's eye to put whatever *kanji* character they like into the name.

In the restaurant, the layers of garden are in the form of trays, stacked, staggered, and layered at different heights in the underground space, with a view from each partitioned table area. The lighting design makes careful use of pools of light from spots within a blackened interior, which adds to the impression of a mysterious space with miniature gardens floating in the air.

Opposite page: Souen is an underground restaurant in Tokyo that offers beautiful "garden" views.

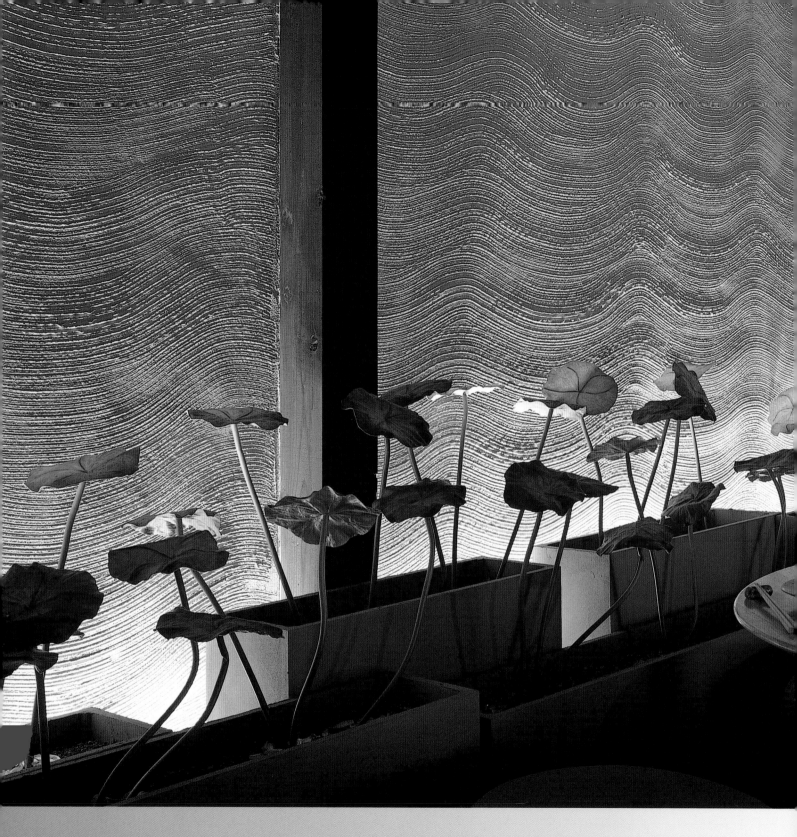

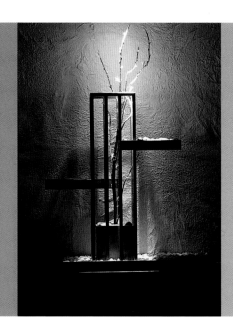

Harada's gardens, which he has also installed on his penthouse terrace at home (illustrated on page 111), are stainless steel trays, mobile and in some cases on wheels. The plantings, if that is the word, feature mainly freeze-dried moss and arrangements of pebbles to give a strange sense of limbo – the moss in a state of suspended animation and the pebbles recalling the Japanese tradition of *karesansui*, or dry-stone garden – all encased in efficient polished steel.

"It would not have been satisfactory to use fake vegetation, such as Astro-turf," says Harada. "The underground space needed to be brought alive by having real moss with its organic quality. The fact that the moss is somehow breathing is a nuance is that is apparent to people, as they certainly have the five senses to feel it." In Japan, the word *iyashi* (healing) is often used to refer to the feeling of relaxation

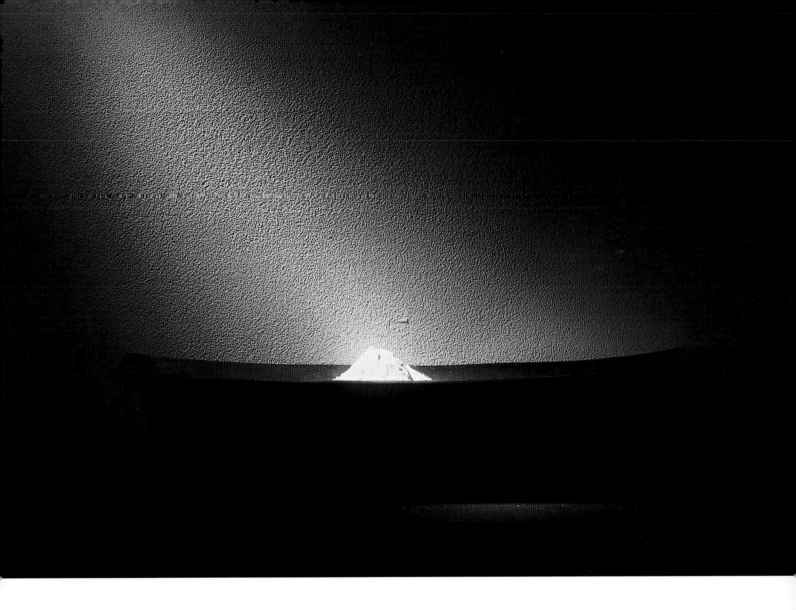

induced by being exposed to nature. Although this may sound like a rather esoteric detail, one of the secrets of this restaurant's success is how well it treats and teases people's senses.

There are 33 individually sectioned rooms at Souen, each seating two people. One of the reasons why a regular clientele has built up since the restaurant's opening in March of 2002, other than the reasonable price, is that each small room has a different view. Combined with the enhanced feeling of spaciousness from the black walls and ceiling, which recede to infinity under the pooled spot-lighting, is the intriguing sense of variety. Customers tend to have an idea for their next visit, a different table with a different view when they return.

The low entrances to these rooms remind the Japanese of the *nijiriguchi* (literally "wriggling-in entrance") of the traditional tea ceremony room. You need to bend down in order to enter; and this kind of anti-everyday space creates a special atmosphere for the sake and the meal. The menu includes top-quality fish and improvisatory dishes such as mixed-rice risotto and spring-rolls containing cream cheese and salmon.

Hatago An element of the success that the Harada/Morii team has enjoyed is due to the input of marketing guru Kawarai. Kawarai, an old friend of Harada's, conducts market research and understands the elements needed for a restaurant to be successful financially as well as from a design and dining perspective. As Harada knows the restaurant guest, Kawarai knows the restaurant owner. With the success of Souen, this trio has further developed the theme of a secluded underground space in a restaurant called Hatago, which opened in August 2002. Here again, there is a sense of a modified "Japanese style", with direct reference to history.

The beauty of this place is how individual space has been successfully emphasized: by using old-fashioned Japanese inn accommodation as a motif, they create the "time" to relax at night. The word *hatago* is an old term, long out of use; originally it meant a horse's feed basket for a journey, then it gradually changed to meaning a basket for people's food and tools. Finally it came to refer to the accommodation at a place where such baskets were gathered. In the Edo period (1457–1590), every post-town (evening stopover between work and home) had numbers of *hatago* lining the streets for travellers.

In the 21st century, a restaurant such as this, located in the heart of Roppongi in downtown Tokyo, is a contemporary *hatago*. For city dwellers, the entertainment districts are the new post-towns. Roppongi, with its nightclubs and bars – a Mecca for foreign travellers, incidentally – is one of the rowdiest; it is known and loved for its noisy energy. Harada and the team here created a space which is much

Right: A dining room at Souen.
Opposite page: The dining rooms at Hatago, another Harada restaurant, this time themed on a traditional traveller's inn. Harada's mobile stone and moss gardens feature in front.

more than a restaurant; it firmly establishes the ambience of a *yado* – an "inn with an impression of quietness" that functions as an oasis of calm. The floor area at Hatago is almost 300 metres square, but there is seating for only 70. There are 16 counter-table seats available for those who want to meet friends for a drink first, and the remainder are all in individual rooms, some of them free-standing. These intentionally resemble tea-ceremony rooms where people can feel comfortable in an enclosed space.

Harada notes that "individual space is a luxury for the Japanese", and typically it is only expensive *ryoutei* (the archetypal traditional Japanese restaurant) that provide a private room. High rental costs prevent the majority of restaurants from offering this. At Hatago, the detached rooms, small buildings in their own right, each fit four people. In some, the seating style is known as *hori-gotatsu* – a *tatami-mat* room, but one in which there is a rectangular pit under the table so that the guests can sit Western fashion, without folding their legs. In other rooms there are *za-buton* (seating cushions) which are specifically designed at a comfortable height for sitting on the floor, in consideration less for Westerners than for young Japanese who are not so used to sitting on a *tatami*-mat.

Opposite page: A waitress serves at a *tatami*-mat room at Hatago. There is a rectangular pit under the table so that the guests can sit Western fashion.
Below left: Yasuhiro Harada has created gardens on top of the detached dining rooms to provide an interesting view to those at a higher level in the restaurant.
Below right: One of the dining rooms even features an *o-furo* (Japanese-style bath), a humorous reference to the inn theme of the restaurant.

When the food is ready, a waitress knocks on the door. The room is not large, but each guest has adequate space without crowding. There is enough space between them so that the guests need not worry that their conversations can be overheard. Best of all, these *hanare* (detached rooms) are mounted on wheels so that, depending on the season, they can be rearranged, completely changing the overall layout. Producing different "post-towns" every now and then was part of the original concept.

The cube gardens, which are located outside the detached private rooms, are another one of Harada's ideas. These gardens are also located on top of the mobile rooms, a great use of space. Though people who are in the "box" (the mobile room) cannot see the garden on their own roof, it can be seen by those who are dining above them at a higher level.

Although this restaurant, with its small seating capacity, might appear luxurious, it actually makes an extremely efficient use of space. These designs are also perfectly suited to the landscape. The varied elevation makes possible different views from different spots. People return frequently to the restaurant not only because the food changes frequently, but because the townscapes vary.

Previous page: The 9.6-metre (31-foot)
bar at the luxurious Secret M bar in Ebisu
Below left: The discreet sign for the bar.
Below right and opposite page: The
unfinished stone wall in M Bar contrasts
with the sleek bar and opulent chandelier
to create an unusual atmosphere.

Secret M An exposed, unfinished wall is a key feature of the "secret" M Bar. This rough stone wall, which would not be striking under sunlight, has been coupled with a chandelier and a halogen light to create a strangely mysterious atmosphere.

In a mocking defiance of the luxuriousness of the restaurant "bubble", the sofas are not brand name collector's items or antiques. The emphasis here is on comfort and, in particular, the comfortable feeling that leather can provide. Nevertheless, the counter is 9.6 metres (31 feet) in length – unusually long for a Japanese site – and contributes to an overall impression that this bar is both grand and gorgeous.

Ebisu, M's location, is a town deconstructed from the inside out. The original character of the town was destroyed by the redevelopment rampant during the country's boom economy in the late 1980s and early 1990s. Its scenery now resembles contemporary Boston – or some of its less attractive sections, at least – transplanted to Japan.

Because of Ebisu's proximity to the business areas of Shibuya and Aoyama, it used to be a heavily residential area. Now it has become something of a sightseeing spot for the younger set, and the families and older adults who were familiar with the quality of the old Ebisu have left. But for the sightseer and the diner, the contradictions of the area – old next to new, evidence of an infusion of money next to what the bubble economy left behind – is a point of interest.

The bar successfully encapsulates the disparities of Ebisu. Entry to the bar is members only, and the cost per head is as high as bars in Ginza at its height (an area famous for its expensive bars and clubs). These marks of luxuriousness are in a sense contradicted by the bar's exterior: no sign is posted outside; a discreet letter "M" is simply posted on the door. And then there is the unbalanced luxury of the interior, with the unpolished wall juxtaposed with the chandelier. These unexpected features have been embraced by its customers and the public, who praise the bar for its sophisticated and successful combination of "roughness and beauty", which suits the new, dichotomous Ebisu.

Hinode Shokudou Yosei Kiyono knows the importance of surprising people. He has managed to do so by creating a restaurant that harks back to a recent era to create a strangely nostalgic and slightly cynical experience. The restaurant Hinode Shokudou is a reproduction of a scene from memory, in this case a scene from Kiyono's childhood. From the 1950s until the early 1970s, Japan began to change its culture by copying the West. Japanese people followed the Western fashion of drinking sparkling soda water; it was considered trendy to be served by a waitress wearing Western clothes rather than by a girl in a kimono. Western movies were a complete luxury at that time, and Kiyono was fascinated by them. Those "twisted" visions of the West changed by the time he grew up, morphing from a view inspired by fantasy to a more realistic picture of Western life.

As Kiyono points out, "Nowadays, we can go to foreign countries ourselves, and can experience them in reality. The importation of European culture at that time by those who had never been there is now seen as kitschy, and that aesthetic is being recreated in the Japanese sensibility." And, of course, for those who were born in the 1980s, it appears to be an entirely new style of design.

Dharma Whereas many of the new Japanese designers approach their projects from a non-conceptual, purely design perspective, the approach for the restaurant Dharma in Ginza took a completely different tack. The design was generated from the question: "What would it be like if a foreigner who has never been to Japan designed a Japanese-style restaurant?" This type of misunderstanding is often seen in film, where stereotypical images of geisha, Mount Fuji, and kamikaze (a word not even known to many Japanese young people) get mixed together with vivid Korean-style colours and a Chinese hanging scroll. The trademark of Dharma's look is a cynical, "anti-Japanese" or "pseudo-Japanese" style. The round doll at the restaurant's entrance is the Daruma-doll (see page 129), a charm that is said to bring good luck and prosperity for businessmen. Traditionally, the doll's colour would be red; here it is portrayed in a Western-like zebra

Above: Yosei Kiyono talks to the chef in Hinode Shokudou, the restaurant he based on Japan's "twisted" vision of the West from the 1950s to 1970s.
Right: Waitresses in Western-style outfits.
Opposite page: Western-influenced advertisements line the walls of Hinode Shokudou.

pattern. The mahjong tiles displayed towards the back of the entranceway are ironic. It is common knowledge to the Japanese that mahjong was imported to Japan from China in the Taisho period. The butterfly in the picture below left slyly refers to the Western association of butterflies with Japan.

There's an unusual room in the restaurant that tends to shock people – in it are displayed *shunga*, erotic woodblock prints from the Edo period. These traditional Japanese *shunga* prints are not usually viewed in public, and the designers looked long and hard to find these rarities. In addition, geishas' names are written on the *chochin* (lanterns) on the ceiling. Clearly, this is a scene which cannot be viewed under usual circumstances.

The irony of Dharma's style illuminates the difference between the younger Japanese generation – a generation extremely aware of how they are perceived in the West – and the preceding generation – a generation who treated Western ideas (and misconceptions) with more deference.

The design originated with a concept by the team of BBA International, and was completed by designer Yoshihisa Matsuzawa. The company specializes in the planning and management of bars, restaurants, and amusement facilities. BBA reflects a tendency in today's Japanese restaurant industry for business and design to come from the same company, unified to create a vision which reflects a new Japanese identity and cosmopolitanism.

Above left: East collides with West at Dharma.
Above right: A traditional *daruma* doll is given a Western zebra-stripe look.

Opposite: A room in Dharma covered with erotic woodblock prints and lanterns with the names of geishas written on them.

Chika Bar The up-and-coming Italian designer Claudio Colucci now lives in Japan. Claudio, a former employee of Philippe Starck, uses Japanese materials and design in an interesting way. Chika Bar is in Kagurazaka, an old-fashioned, almost anachronistic neighbourhood in Tokyo. Here, unlike the rest of modern, urban Japan, the streets are still narrow, and one can find many *ryoutei* (traditional Japanese restaurants) nearby. The local residents take a certain pride in this preserved urban landscape and they resist its modernization.

The owner of the Chika Bar, Chika, has been a geisha for many years and she had long held dreams of running her own establishment. The original structure of Chika Bar was built soon after the end of the Second World War and was once the home of a shiatsu masseur. When it came time to refurbish the house, Chika went to Claudio Colucci. Since the house is made of wood, and is over 50 years old, Colucci had to be careful not to destabilize the existing structure. He first removed the walls dividing the living space and the work (massage room) space. While the massage room (with a *tatami* mat used for shiatsu) was kept pretty much as it was, the rest of the space was completely reanimated.

Previous page: Chika Bar is a modern bar created within a traditional house in the heart of one of Tokyo's most old-fashioned neighbourhoods.
Above: The sign for Chika Bar.
Opposite page and right: The LED lighting, a trademark of Italian designer Claudio Colucci, creates a futuristic feel.

Colucci installed an LED (light emitting diode) lighting system in the bar area, creating a futuristic atmosphere. The bar counter itself is made from a slim coloured tube. An incandescent lamp and a halogen light fixed into the ceiling provide further lighting. Colucci's intention in keeping the massage room with the *tatami* mat intact was to represent the past. His idea was to create a continuum of time extending from the past towards the future – from the *tatami* mat to the bar counter. An old heavy chest of drawers, left by the *shiatsu-shi* (masseur), looms oppressively in the room, giving the feeling of an evocative stage set. It is almost as if the chest is a prop from the past that mysteriously propels us into the future.

The polycarbinate covering the LED lighting at the bar is 3mm ($\frac{1}{2}$ in) thick. Also designed by Claudio, this covering causes a subtle shift in colour and atmosphere over a 30-minute period. Claudio believes that the LED lighting "brings both brightness and feeling to the bar, thus creating an intellectually engaged landscape". Colucci's lighting certainly brings new life to a historical building.

Below left: An ingenious wine glass
at Moph.
Below right: Two phases from Colucci's
subtly shifting LED light display at Moph.

Opposite page: Exploring the theme of
morphing (hence the café's name) Colucci
designed table legs that change in section
from square to circular and back again.

Moph Claudio first used this LED lighting system in a café on a park road in Shibuya, a trendier neighborhood than Kagurazaka. The café's name, Moph, comes from the English word "morph". Claudio designed furniture for Moph that explores basic design concepts that can be expanded upon and repeated. A table leg that is square at the top changes gradually to become a cylinder, and then slowly becomes square once again. Claudio has studied sociology, aesthetics, and philosophy; he considers design questions at the most fundamental levels. "Why is a circle a circle, and the square a square? What is the meaning of these shapes? Why do the majority of tables have four legs?" Colucci's designs address conscious and subconscious perceptions. The psychological effects are achieved through careful control of his materials. For example, the colours in his subtly changing LED lighting scheme were chosen from over 16,700,000 available from Color Kinetics, an American firm, to create a "Mediterranean" feeling.

"I was surprised by the gap between my expectations and the reality that I experienced when I first came to Japan,"Claudio notes. "It is not necessarily a negative thing. The first concepts I learned in Japan were 'cute', 'happy', and 'colourful' – the world and words of young girls. I then became aware of the different eras of Japanese history, and learned about the designers of previous generations, although I had relatively little exposure to exotic art such as Urushi and Kimono art. It became apparent to me that as technology advanced, the Japanese changed both their lifestyle and their sense of identity."

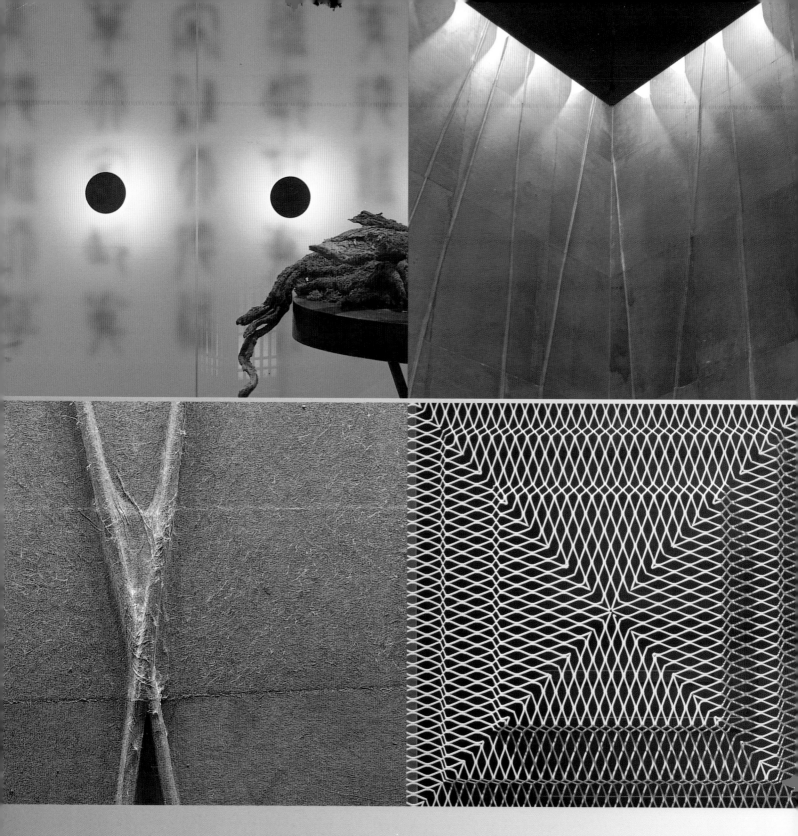

Clockwise from top left: Zassou-ya, An Aburiyaki & Sushi Restaurant, An Aburiyaki & Sushi

Restaurant, Royal, Kowloon Dimsum, Dharma, BEAMS HOUSE, An Aburiyaki & Sushi Restaurant.

Royal Hisae Igarashi, designer of Body Relax Fuu (page 78) and the Tango Chest (page 92) has created a chic American-style restaurant, but with a calm, Japanese-style ambience. Royal is a restaurant in Harajyuki, a prime and bustling area of the city where the newest thing can be found. This is not a residential district, and there is a frequent turnover of businesses. Many designers and sophisticated, creative professionals have offices among the shops in Harajyuki. Tourists and young people come to shop here for fashionable clothes and accessories. Needless to say, it's not easy to create a popular restaurant for this sophisticated crowd, but that's just what the owner aimed to do.

Royal has succeeded in good part because of its comfortable atmosphere. Normally, in a high-rent district such as this, an owner would not want to encourage customers to stay for a long time; but Royal encourages its patrons to linger. The bench seating creates an American feel, but the décor has Japanese references: the colour scheme is a chic beige, and the surfaces are vinyl-leather and plywood. The bare plywood calls to mind Japanese plain wood, and creates a peaceful ambience. The lighting, calibrated to harmonize with the wood, was also designed by Igarashi. According to Igarashi, "Wood has a presence and power that is sensed even when it is not visible. Even when wood surfaces are painted with metallic paint, the wood maintains its identity; somehow it doesn't completely disappear. Because of this presence, wood can be difficult to handle. But it was important to have wood furniture in the space – it brings a 'soft' quality that is necessary."

The floor and ceiling are made from harder materials: metal and concrete. The balance between metal, concrete, and wood works well, the contrasts highlighting the qualities of the different materials. Details have been added to attract the target clientele, such as a small light that Hisae Igarashi designed and installed in the smart interior. Shaped like a brooch and installed with a photo, this "cute" little light goes straight to the hearts of the high-school girls who come to dine.

Opposite (far left): The entrance to
Royal, a restaurant in Tokyo's bustling
Harajyuki, designed by Hisae Igarashi.
Opposite (left): Royal combines American
themes with a Japanese approach to
colour scheme and materials.
Above: Hisae Igarashi also designed the
lighting at Royal to harmonize with the
plywood surfaces.
Overleaf: J-pop Café, an audio-visual
insight into Japanese pop culture.

J-pop Café For a comfortable vibe and excellent music, J-pop café in Shibuya is hard to beat. Its interior is designed specifically for listening to music – Japanese pop music, the only music played at J-pop. Under the domed roof there are 16 projection screens so that people can enjoy both music and film simultaneously. If privacy is desired, it's possible to borrow one's favourite CDs and play them in private rooms or booths. The interior is a mixture of the past and the present, with furniture from the mid-century: the 1950s and 1960s.

BBA International is the "producer" of this café as well as Dharma. Whereas Dharma re-envisioned Japanese culture through Western eyes, cafés such as J-pop are introducing a truer representation of today's Japanese pop culture – in music, film, fashion, cuisine – to the outside world.

"Mid-century culture is popular in Japan now," comments designer Matsuzawa. "The interior from the film *A Clockwork Orange* is an example. We want to export these fashions via Japan, through a Japanese lens rather than only through that of the United States or Europe, with our Japanese music."

Matsuzawa does not come from a design background; he initially worked in the catering industry during the recent boom times in the restaurant business. His experience working at the "front of the house", interacting directly with customers, led him towards the goal of creating "comfortable design". He learned that novelty for novelty's sake can become boring, and that customers can tire of concepts being pushed upon them by the designer.

Opposite page: The reception at J-pop Café. The designer, Matsuzawa, cites 1960s films such as *A Clockwork Orange* as an influence.
Below: Private listening booths where customers can borrow their favourite CDs to listen to.

Above: Toraji is a Korean restaurant
designed with a Western feel by
Yukio Hashimoto.
Opposite page: The Hangul lettering on
the walls is the sole Korean motif in the
restaurant (it spells out a recipe for *kim
chi*, the Korean national dish).

Toraji This Korean restaurant, opened in autumn 2002, mixes Western motifs with Asian style. Toraji is located in the Maru Building, a landmark in Marunouchi, a business district in Tokyo near the train station. The renewal of the Maru Building in 2002 was a much anticipated event. Its rents had skyrocketed during the economic bubble and tenants in the building began to have trouble paying them. Large brand-name companies started moving out, more fashionable (and fashion-related) businesses started moving in, and the building began to take on a new identity in Tokyo.

Integral to the successful transformation of the Marunouchi district was the change in character of the restaurants in and around the Maru Building. To succeed, restauranteurs had to attract the business of the fashionable women coming to this part of the city. Toraji's success comes from its clever blend of old and new, Western and Asian. It serves authentic Korean food, but its interior palette has a Western-type feel. Yukio Hashimoto's design is based on white colours and natural light.

Hashimoto says that "it is not enough just to return to old-style Japanese imagery", such as designs that only use bamboo. It would not be convincing for this generation. He thinks that successful future designs must not only be expressions of reality and naturalism but also that, to be relevant, design must reflect contemporary lifestyles. The combination of European décor and Hangul (Korean) characters creates a contemporary synergy linking the past to the future. Hashimoto's design is a style in which two entirely different cultures can naturally live together.

The restaurant's overall aim is to create an inviting, café-like atmosphere for its young, predominantly female customers. The Hangul letters (which can be viewed as a graphic installation) are the only visual elements with specifically Korean motifs. They are not intended to reproduce Korean style per se, but to reflect the vital cosmopolitan energy of the Maru-no-uchi area.

Zassou-ya Hashimoto wants to "create an overall atmosphere, not just make physical changes to a space". He has created another Korean restaurant, Zassou-ya, which is inspired by temples that were built in Korea's Tempyo period. The faded colours chosen by Hashimoto evoke the temples' aged look, a change in atmosphere from the restaurant's immediate past as a club.

Zassou-ya is located in a high-price residential area, not far from Roppongi. There are quite a large number of design studios and offices nearby, and the overall style of the area is fashionable and sophisticated. To be successful in this neighbourhood, the restaurant needed to be equally sophisticated, and Hisae Igarashi, the designer of Royal, was brought in to help achieve a relaxed and tranquil atmosphere.

Zassou-ya's high ceilings from its days as a club were kept as they were. They contrast with the low height of the "jumping" door, which is one of the first things you notice upon entering. In Japan, a door's height is about 180cm (72in), but this door is in the shorter Korean style and you can easily hit your head if you are not careful. This unusual combination of high ceiling and short door provides a surreal, disorienting effect.

The manager of Zassou-ya mentions that "In general, Korean restaurant designers place little emphasis on creating special effects for characteristic interiors. But this place attempts to create a feeling of Korean identity by focusing on the image of their temples." And careful attention to detail is also used to great effect, even in places one would not normally look for such detail. For example, the paper on the floor is coated with wax, subtly drawing attention to the materials employed in creating the temple atmosphere.

An Aburiyaki & Sushi Restaurant In Japan's restaurant industry, there is a saying that can be translated as "one-stop style", in which a building (or one floor of a building) contains the combined functions of a restaurant and bar and different elements of style – all in one. XEX Daikanyama is an extreme example of this. One floor of this building not only houses An Aburiyaki & Sushi restaurant, but also a Neapolitan-style Italian restaurant, a New York-style bar, and a swimming pool with a Bali-style dining area next to it.

It was important not to overdecorate each of the four environments since they are located right next to each other. Designed by the team of Ichiro Shiomi and Etsuko Yamamoto, known collectively as Spin-off, the An Aburiyaki & Sushi restaurant attempts to create a

voluminous expansive feeling within a Japanese space. To avoid a sense of cultural confusion, the designers combined minimalist decoration with a bold use of layout.

The food served is Japanese cuisine: An has the feel of the historic town Gion in Kyoto. The use of real bamboo covered with Japanese paper on one section of the wall creates the intriguing feeling of being both outdoors and indoors at the same time.

When designing the counter area, the designer's challenge was again to make sure "not to overdecorate". In order to emphasize the simple beauty and functionality of the shelves, they are kept simple. "To create a sense of unity between the Italian, New York, and Bali restaurants it was important to pay attention to the unity of the entire space, and not just focus on particulars like colour scheme. The high ceiling provided an advantage in that one can create a feeling of Kyoto alleyways, with changes around the corner," say the Spinoff designers. And so when one moves into the bar area, one feels that a natural transition has been made. As Michimasa Kawaguchi states

Opposite page and below: The An Japanese restaurant, one of a group of international restaurants located on a floor of the XEX Daikanyama building. To minimize cultural clashes, the designers, Spin-off, merely hint at a Japanese identity (the paper-covered bamboo on the walls, for example).

in the introduction, these types of shifts in style and culture are made possible because the "younger generation is not limited by a pure definition of authentic Japanese style".

Kowloon Dimsum Japanese designers have begun to free themselves from the shackles of realism and tradition. The designers of Hashimoto's Korean Restaurant, An, and Hinode Shokudou are not trying to reproduce faithful representations of Korea, Italy, New York, or old Japan; their designs are reflections of the images that people have of such places. The Japanese people's love for other places has taken on its own meaning – many times supplanting an interest in the places themselves.

Using the crowded streets of Hong Kong as an inspiration, designer Tsutomu Kurokawa designed Kowloon Dimsum to evoke China without using direct Chinese references such as Chinese furniture or vases. Instead, he incorporated things that are Chinese-like. For example, he printed Chinese traditional patterns that are intentionally turned upside-down, and then placed them on grass walls. "Imperfection makes you feel comfortable," he says.

Next door is Cool Chang, a Thai restaurant. When he agreed to design this restaurant, Kurokawa decided not to do any research into Thailand. "I decided to design the restaurant based on the knowledge and image of Thailand that I had at the moment. In my mind's eye,

Opposite page: Two views of Kowloon Dimsum, a Chinese restaurant designed by Tsutomu Kurokawa. Kurokawa's intention was to evoke China without using any specifically Chinese references. *Above:* Kurokawa was equally free when designing the Thai restaurant next door, Cool Chang, basing the look on purely on his preconceptions about Thailand.

Thailand's actual interior is not colourful – even though the temples and the priest's robes are, of course, vividly colourful. So I decided to use only the colour green, to make it look like a lotus."

Sage de Cret Kurokawa wanted to design a boutique that would become even more attractive as it aged, rather than one that would become obsolete as soon as a little dirt appeared on a massive white wall. Sage de Cret, with a design by Kurokawa that reflects his ideas about imperfection, is a boutique for men that is famous among young people in their twenties.

Sage de Cret is located in the pleasant and quiet upscale residential district of Aoyama. Kurokawa thinks that "Japanese shop design is

the most advanced in the world. But when it comes to furniture, European design is probably superior to that of the Japanese. European design is in many ways self-referential, with no nods to Japanese or American design. But I wanted to achieve a new atmosphere by being inclusive and combining characteristics of Japanese architecture with elements of European architecture. Japanese architecture is characteristically light, clean and low-maintenance and uses granite and stainless steel, whereas the stereotypical European architecture is a grey, stone house with dim light."

Kurokawa aimed for a design that had a non-committal, neutral nationality, neither Asian nor European. He combined elements of lightness, cleanliness, gravitas, and low light to create a balanced atmosphere. For example, the hard concrete surfaces of Sage de Cret neutralize the smooth curved line of the stairway. Kurokawa's design is analogous to collecting uneven objects and placing them in a box with a smooth surfaces.

Opposite : Three views of Sage de Cret, a boutique designed by Kurokawa that merges characteristics of Japanese and European architecture.
Below: Maty LED lights designed by Kurokawa, which also feature in the Gallery de Pop (page 31).

Overleaf: Sage de Cret is an illustration of Kurokawa's ideas of imperfection – it was designed to become more attractive as it ages.

BEAMS HOUSE The design of BEAMS expresses both the formality and stature of European architecture and the lightness of modern Japanese architecture. BEAMS HOUSE is located on the ground floor of the Maru Building (near the Korean restaurant Toraji); it has become one of the most famous and exclusive shops in all of Japan. The store carries fashion items selected from all over the world, as well as a line of original products; their stock manages to combine nostalgia with modernism.

Yukio Hashimoto, the designer of BEAMS HOUSE has created a sort of modern mansion here. By covering the walls with expanded metal lathing, an expression of his respect for European history and architecture, Hashimoto has evoked the feel of an old European mansion. But he infuses a modern flow of line into his classical references. "Designs by Frank Lloyd Wright manage to be both classic

Opposite page: A display window at
BEAMS HOUSE, a famous boutique
designed by Yukio Hashimoto, located in
the Maru building.
Right and below: Examples of the varied
lighting at BEAMS and the use of
expanded steel lathing which unifies the
design of the store.

and modern; they never get worn out, or feel out of fashion. His designs are always in my mind," says Hashimoto. The Maru Building is a meeting point of classic and futuristic style, and the selection of products and materials at BEAMS reflects this same combination. Hashimoto uses expanded metal lathing everywhere to unify the whole shop. Different parts of the store are modelled after different rooms in a mansion. The checkout counter looks like the front desk of an imaginary hotel.

As one walks through the store, from the men's section to the lady's section, and through the passageways, the lighting changes, and creates an optical illusion that one is in a place that is larger than its actual size. Hashimoto's mansion becomes a magical one that expands room to room as you move though it.

Page numbers in *italic* refer to illustrations and captions

Acknowledgments

The author would like to thank the following people for their help with this project:

Takeshi Yoneshima/Kumi Aizawa/Hikaru Soga/Ikuko Kaitani/Tomomichi Natsume/Jun Yamaguchi/Jun Terashima/Takuya Nakamura/Hiromi Egoshi/Mika Shono/Marie Don Seki/Macky Fukuda/Mie Katayose/Yudai Tachikawa/Kazuhiko Kamiyama/Yuka Kikuchi/Masako Yamagami/Atsushi Morimura/Kimie Hoshino/Kayoko Yamamura/Kazuhiko Tsuchida/Yutaka Maeda Hideki Kishino/Kiyoshi Kimura/Shinpei Tokitsu/Kimitoshi Chida/Shuku Miura/Takehiko Umemura/Shiro Kobayashi/Tomotoki Osaki/Chika Muto/Shin Kawamura/Mayu Yoshikawa/Ikuko Shigeta

Thanks also to Kozo Takayama, who took the photographs of Tsutomu Kurokawa's Lenorat lights featured on pages 65 and 94–5.